Tutorial for JBuilder

Y. Daniel Liang

An Alan R. Apt Book

PEARSON
Prentice
Hall

Pearson Education, Inc.
Upper Saddle River, New Jersey 07458

Library of Congress Cataloging-in-Publication Data

CIP data on file

Vice President and Editorial Director, ECS: *Marcia Horton*
Publisher: *Alan R. Apt*
Associate Editor: *Toni D. Holm*
Editorial Assistant: *Patrick Lindner*
Vice President and Director of Production and Manufacturing, ESM: *David W. Riccardi*
Executive Managing Editor: *Vince O'Brien*
Assistant Managing Editor: *Camille Trentacoste*
Production Editor: *Lakshmi Balasubramanian*
Director of Creative Services: *Paul Belfanti*
Art Director: *Jayne Conte*
Cover Designer: *Bruce Kenselaar*
Art Editor: *Gregory Dulles*
Manufacturing Manager: *Trudy Pisciotti*
Manufacturing Buyer: *Lisa McDowell*
Marketing Manager: *Pamela Shaffer*
Marketing Assistant: *Barrie Reinhold*

© 2004 Pearson Education, Inc.
Pearson Prentice Hall
Upper Saddle River, NJ 07458

The author and publisher of this book have used their best efforts in preparing this book. These efforts
include the development, research, and testing of the theories and programs to determine their
effectiveness. The author and publisher make no warranty of any kind, expressed or implied, with regard
to these programs or the documentation contained in this book. The author and publisher shall not be
liable in any event for incidental or consequential damages in connection with, or arising out of, the
furnishing, performance, or use of these programs.

Printed in the United States of America

10 9 8 7 6 5 4 3 2 1

ISBN 0-13-141079-2

Pearson Education Ltd., *London*
Pearson Education Australia Pty. Ltd., *Sydney*
Pearson Education Singapore, Pte. Ltd.
Pearson Education North Asia Ltd., *Hong Kong*
Pearson Education Canada, Inc., *Toronto*
Pearson Educatión de Mexico, S.A. de C.V.
Pearson Education—Japan, *Tokyo*
Pearson Education Malaysia, Pte. Ltd.
Pearson Education, Inc., *Upper Saddle River, New Jersey*

To Samantha, Michael, and Michelle

Preface

This book is written for students who are currently taking a Java course that uses JBuilder and for Java programmers who want to develop Java projects using JBuilder.

You can use Java 2 SDK to write Java programs. Java 2 SDK (formerly known as JDK) consists of a set of separate programs, such as compiler and interpreter, each of which is invoked from a command line. Besides Java 2 SDK, there are more than a dozen Java development tools on the market today, including Borland JBuilder, Sun ONE Studio (formerly known as Forte for Java), IBM Visual Age for Java, and Web-Gain Visual Café. These tools support an *integrated development environment* (IDE) for rapidly developing Java programs. Editing, compiling, building, debugging, and on-line help are integrated in one graphical user interface. Using these tools effectively will greatly increase your programming productivity.

This book introduces JBuilder. Produced by Borland, JBuilder is a premier Java development tool for developing Java programs. Over the years, Borland has led the charge in creating visual development tools like Delphi and C++ Builder. The first edition of JBuilder was released in September 1997. Over a short time JBuilder has been improved rapidly. The newest edition is JBuilder 8. Since JBuilder 3.5, JBuilder has been written completely in Java. It uses the Swing component library, provided by JavaSoft (Sun Microsystems), as its foundation. This pure Java component library allows JBuilder to have a sophisticated user interface and remain 100% Java. The Swing library also gives the added benefit of a pluggable look-and-feel, which allows JBuilder to adjust its appearance to match the computer's native operating system UI without sacrificing the power and flexibility of the JBuilder UI. JBuilder runs on the Windows 98, NT, and 2000, Mac, Linux, and Solaris platforms.

This tutorial is based on JBuilder 8, which is available in three editions: JBuilder Personal, JBuilder Standard, and JBuilder Enterprise.

- *JBuilder Personal* is ideal for beginners to learn the basics of Java programming. It can be downloaded free for educational use from *www.borland.com*.
- *JBuilder Standard* contains the essential components for developing Java applications and applets. It also contains the Borland JavaBeans components for creating database applications.
- *JBuilder Enterprise* contains all the components in JBuilder Standard, plus support for creating distributed applications using CORBA, and for creating Web applications using Java servlets, Java Server Pages, and XML.

> *Note*: JBuilder Foundation was renamed JBuilder Personal after JBuilder 5, and JBuilder Professional was rebranded as JBuilder Standard after JBuilder 7.

> *Note*: The tutorial is based on JBuilder 8. However, you can also use it with JBuilder 4/5/6/7, since all these editions have the same user interface and very similar features.

About the Author

Y. Daniel Liang is the author and editor of the Prentice-Hall Liang Java Series. Dr. Liang is currently a Yamacraw professor of software engineering in the School of Computing at Armstrong Atlantic State University, Savannah, Georgia. He can be reached at liang@armstrong.edu.

Acknowledgments

I would like to thank Ray Greenlaw and Armstrong Atlantic State University for enabling me to teach what I write and for supporting me in writing what I teach. Teaching is the source of inspiration for the book. I am grateful to the students and instructors who have offered comments, suggestions, bug reports, and praise. Their enthusiastic support has contributed to the success of my books.

I would like to thank Alan Apt, Toni Holm, Patrick Lindner, Lakshmi Balasubramanian, Xiaohong Zhu, Jake Warde, Pamela Shaffer Barrie Reinhold, and their colleagues at Prentice-Hall for organizing, managing, and producing this book.

As always, I am indebted to my wife, Samantha, for love, support, and encouragement.

Table of Contents

Companion Web Site for the Book

The companion Web site for the book can be accessed from *www.cs.armstrong.edu/liang/jbtutorial.html*. The Web site contains the following resources:

Obtaining and Installing JBuilder 8
HTML Tutorial
Errata
Useful Links
FAQs

CHAPTER 1

Getting Started with JBuilder

Assume you have successfully installed JBuilder on your machine. Start JBuilder from Windows, Solaris, Linux, or Mac. The main JBuilder user interface appears, as shown in Figure 1.1. If you don't see the Welcome project, choose Welcome Project (Sample) from the Help menu.

project pane   main toolbar   file tab

     project toolbar   main menu   content pane(showing the editor)

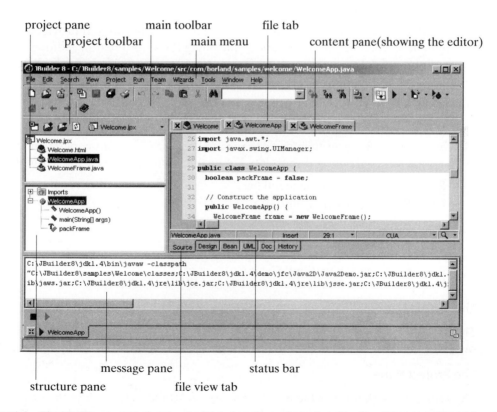

     message pane   status bar

structure pane   file view tab

Figure 1.1   *The JBuilder user interface is a single window that performs functions for editing, compiling, debugging, and running programs.*

Note: The screen shots in this book are from JBuilder 8 Enterprise. *If you use JBuilder 8 Personal or JBuilder 8 Standard, your screen may look slightly different.*

The JBuilder user interface presents a single window for managing Java projects, browsing files, compiling, running, and debugging programs. This user interface has been called *AppBrowser* since JBuilder 3.5. Note that the AppBrowser window and the main window are two separate windows in JBuilder 3, but have been combined into one window since JBuilder 3.5.

Traditional IDE tools use many windows to accommodate various development tasks, such as editing, debugging, and browsing information. As a result, finding the window you need is often difficult. Because it is easy to get lost, beginners may be intimidated. For this reason, some new programmers prefer to use separate utilities, such as the JDK command-line tools, for developing programs.

Borland is aware of the usability problem and has made a significant effort to simplify the JBuilder user interface. JBuilder introduces the AppBrowser window, which enables you to explore, edit, design, and debug projects all in one unified window.

The AppBrowser window primarily consists of the main menu, main toolbar, status bar, project pane, structure pane, and content pane.

1.1   The Main Menu

The main menu is similar to that of other Windows applications and provides most of the commands you need to use JBuilder, including those for creating, editing, compiling, running, and debugging programs. The menu items are enabled and disabled in response to the current context.

1.2   The Toolbar

The toolbar provides buttons for several frequently used commands on the menu bar. Clicking a toolbar is faster than using the menu bar. For some commands, you also can use function keys or keyboard shortcuts. For example, you can save a file in three ways:

- Select *File*, *Save* from the menu bar.
- Click the "save" toolbar button.
- Use the keyboard shortcut Ctrl+S.

Tip: You can display a label, known as *ToolTip*, for a button by pointing the mouse to the button without clicking.

1.3   The Status Bar

The status bar displays a message that alerts the user to the operation status, such as file saved for the Save file command and compilation successful for the Compile command.

1.4   The Project Pane

The *project pane* (known as the *navigation pane* in JBuilder 3) displays the contents of one or more projects opened in the AppBrowser. It consists of the following items, as shown in Figure 1.2.

Figure 1.2   *The project pane manages JBuilder projects.*

- A small toolbar with four buttons (Close Project ![icon], Add To Project ![icon], Remove From Project ![icon], and Refresh ![icon]).
- A drop-down list of all opened projects.
- A tree view of all the files that make up the active project.

The project pane shows a list of one or more files. The project (.jpx) file appears first. Attached to it is a list of the files in the project. The list can include .java, .html, text, or image files. You select a file in the project pane by clicking it. The content pane and the structure pane display information about the selected file. As you select different files in the project pane, each one will be represented in the content and structure panes.

The project pane shown in Figure 1.2 contains three files. The Add button is used to add new files to the project, and the Remove button to remove files from the project. For example, you can remove Welcome.html by selecting the file in the project pane and clicking the Remove button. You can then add the file back to the project as follows:

1. Click the Add button to display the Open dialog box shown in Figure 1.3.
2. Open Welcome.html. You will see Welcome.html displayed in the project pane.

> *Tip*: You can select multiple files by clicking the files with the CTRL key pressed, or select consecutive files with the SHIFT key pressed.

1.5 The Content Pane

The content pane displays all the opened files as a set of tabs. To open a file in the content pane, double-click it in the project pane. The content pane displays the detailed content of the selected file. The editor or viewer used is determined by the file's extension. If you click the WelcomeApp.java file in the project pane, for example, you will see six tabs (Source, Design, Bean, UML, Doc, and History) at the bottom of the content pane (see Figure 1.1). If you select the Source tab, you will see the JBuilder Java source code editor. This is a full-featured, syntax-highlighted programming editor.

If you select Welcome.html in the project pane, you will see the content pane become an HTML browser, as shown in Figure 1.4. If you choose the Source tab, you can view and edit the HTML code in the content pane, as shown in Figure 1.5.

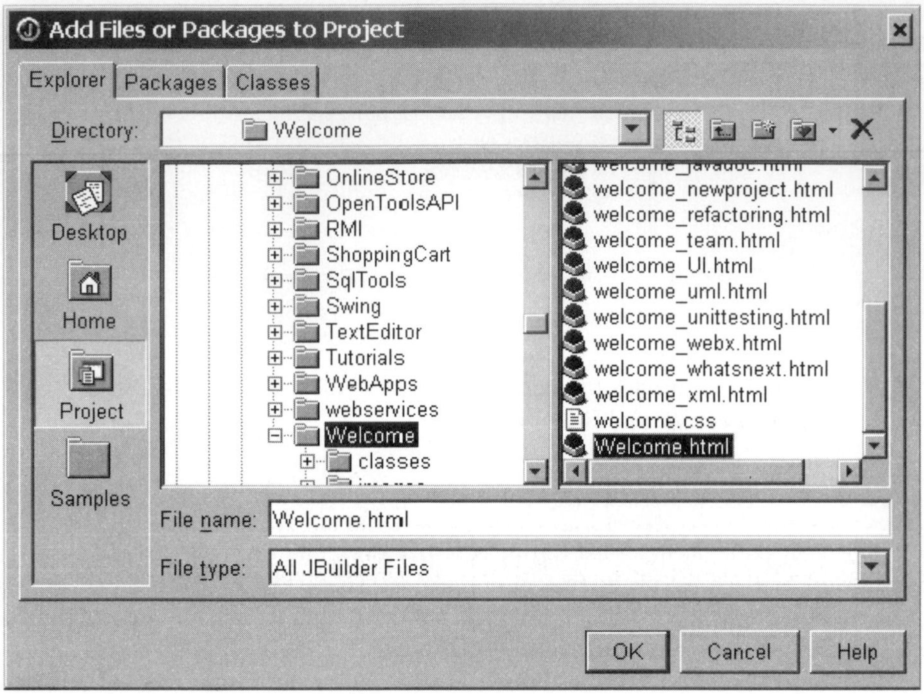

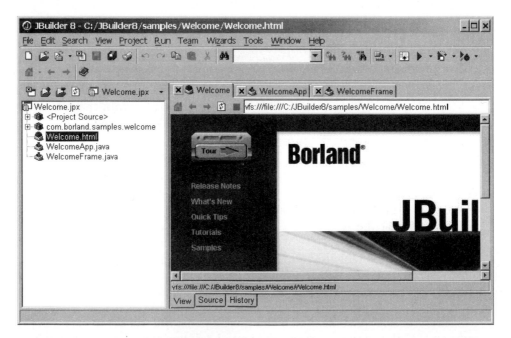

Figure 1.3   *The Open dialog box enables you to open an existing file.*

Figure 1.4   *JBuilder renders HTML files in the content pane.*

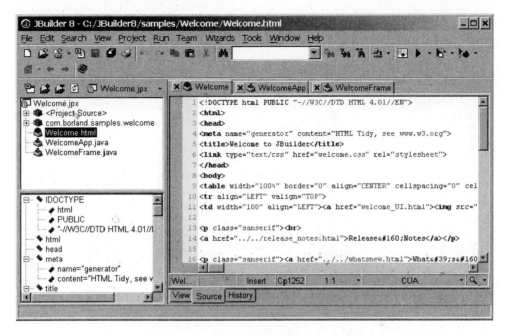

Figure 1.5 *You can edit HTML files in the content pane.*

1.6 The Structure Pane

The *structure pane* displays the structural information about the files you selected in the project pane. All the items displayed in the structure pane are in the form of a hierarchical indexed list. The expand symbol in front of an item indicates that it contains subitems. You can see the subitems by clicking on the expand symbol.

You can also use the structure pane as a quick navigational tool to the various structural elements in the file. If you select the WelcomeFrame.java file, for example, you will see classes, variables, and methods in the structure pane. If you then click on any of those elements in the structure pane, the content pane will move to and highlight it in the source code.

If you click on the **jMenuFile** item in the structure pane, as shown in Figure 1.6, the content pane moves to and highlights the statement that defines the **jMenuFile** data field. This provides a much faster way to browse and find the elements of a file than scrolling through it.

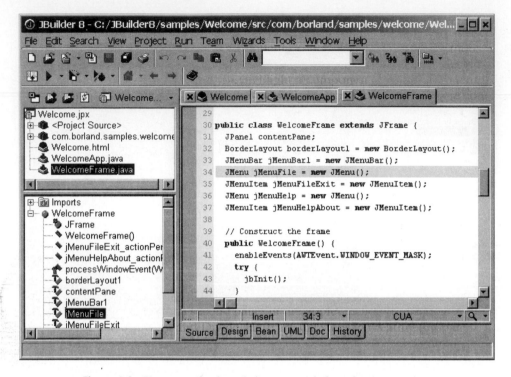

Figure 1.6 *You can cruise through the source code from the structure pane.*

CHAPTER 2

Creating and Managing Projects

A project is like a holder that ties all the files together. The information about each JBuilder project is stored in a project file with a .jpx file extension. (Prior to JBuilder 7, the project file extension was either .jpx or .jpr. The .jpr project files are still compatible in JBuilder 7/8.) The project file contains a list of all the files and project settings and properties. JBuilder uses this information to load and save all the files in the project and compile and run the programs. To create and run a program, you have to first create a project.

2.1   Creating a Project

To avoid frustrating mistakes, it is important to create projects in a consistent and uniform way for all your programs. I recommend that new users create a project as follows:

1. Choose *File, New Project* to bring up the Project wizard dialog box, as shown in Figure 2.1.
2. Type **tutorial** in the Name field and **c:/liang** in the Directory field. Check the *Generate project notes file* option box. Click *Next* to display Project Wizard Step 2 of 3, as shown in Figure 2.2.
3. Type **c:/liang** in the Output path field, **c:/liang/bak** in the Backup path field, and **c:/liang** in the Working directory field. In the Source tab, change the Default path and Test path to **c:/liang**. To do so, click the *Edit* button to display the Select Directory dialog box, as shown in Figure 2.3. Type **c:/liang** in the Directory field. If the directory does not exist, you will see the No Such Directory dialog box, as shown in Figure 2.4. Click *Yes* to return to Project Wizard Step 2 of 3.

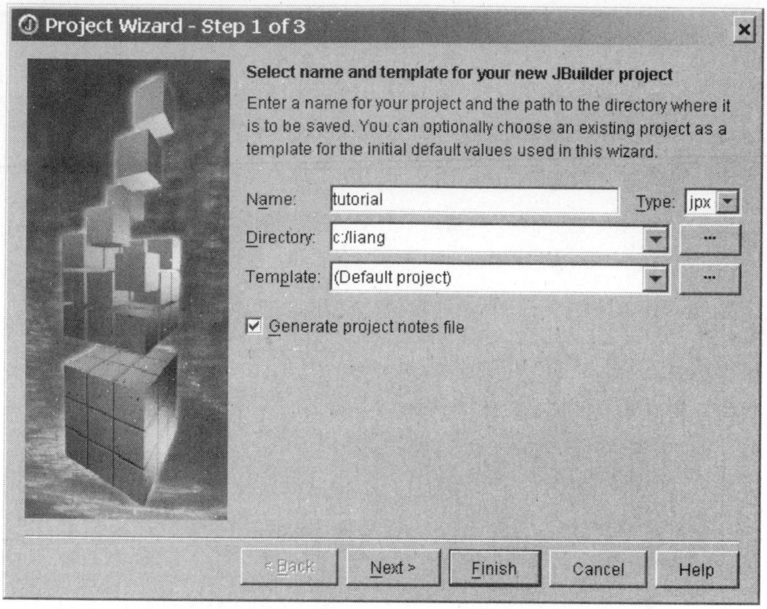

Figure 2.1 *The Project wizard dialog box enables you to specify the project file with other optional information.*

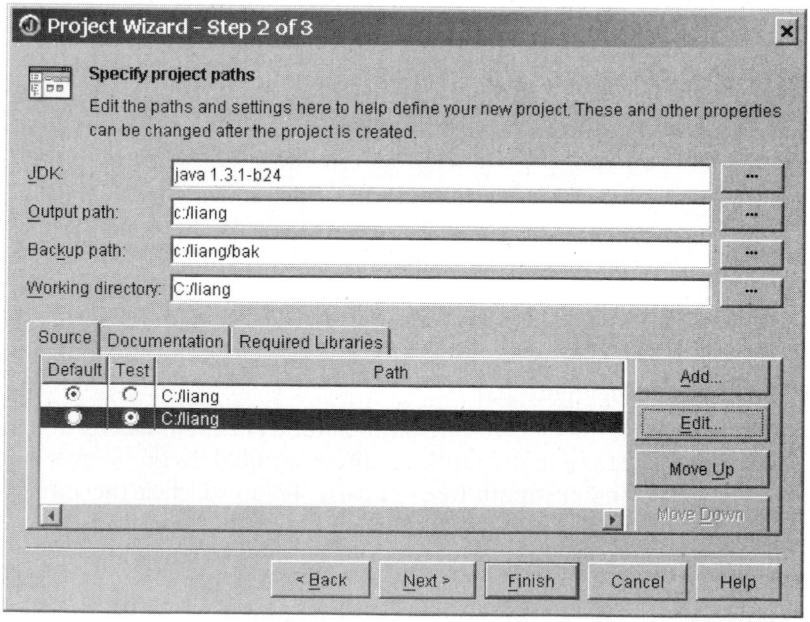

Figure 2.2 *Project Wizard—Step 2 of 3 enables you to modify project settings.*

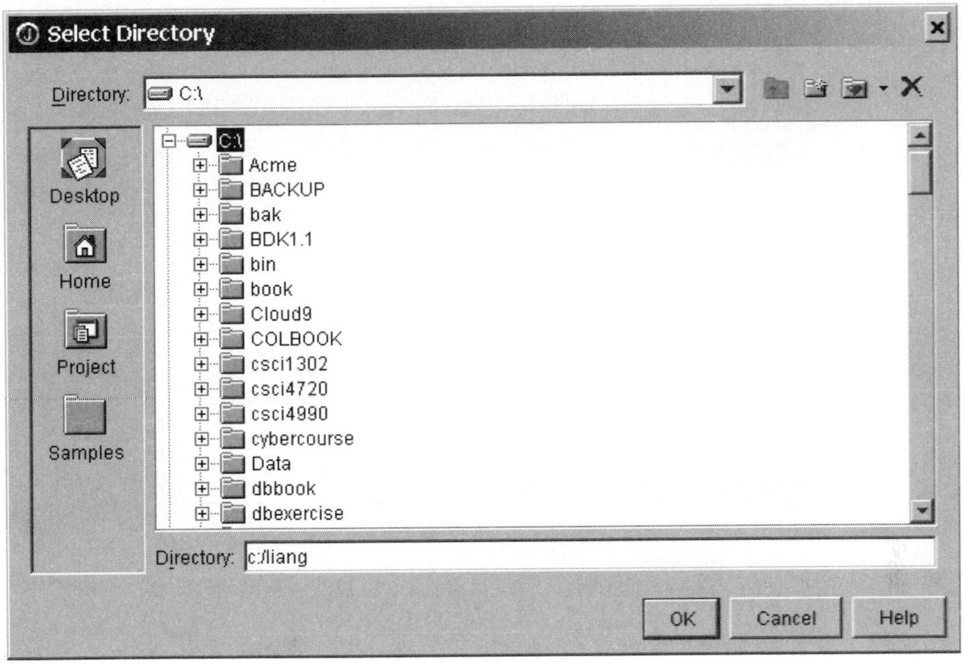

Figure 2.3   *You can select or specify a directory in the Select Directory dialog box.*

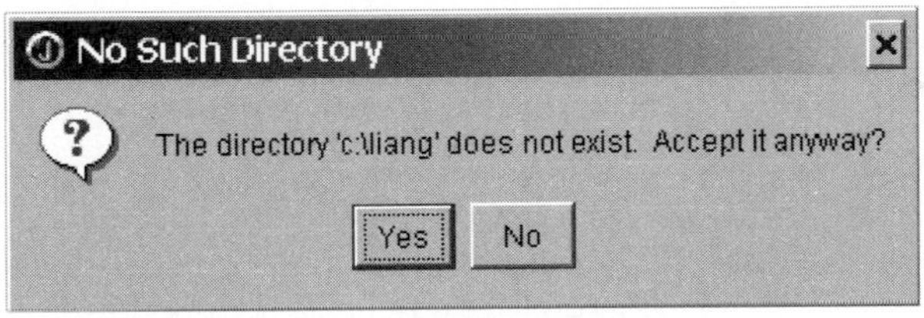

Figure 2.4   *You can select or specify a directory in the Select Directory dialog box.*

4. Click *Next* in Project Wizard Step 2 of 3 to display Project Wizard Step 3 of 3, as shown in Figure 2.5. Fill in the title, author, company, and description fields. These optional fields provide a description for the project.

5. Click *Finish*. The new project is displayed in the project pane, as shown in Figure 2.6. The Project wizard created the project file (tutorial.jpx) and an HTML file (tutorial.html), and placed them in c:\liang. The project file stores the information about the project, and the HTML file is used to describe the project.

> *Note*: JBuilder automatically generates many backup files. I use **bak** as the root directory for all these backup files so that they can be easily located and removed.

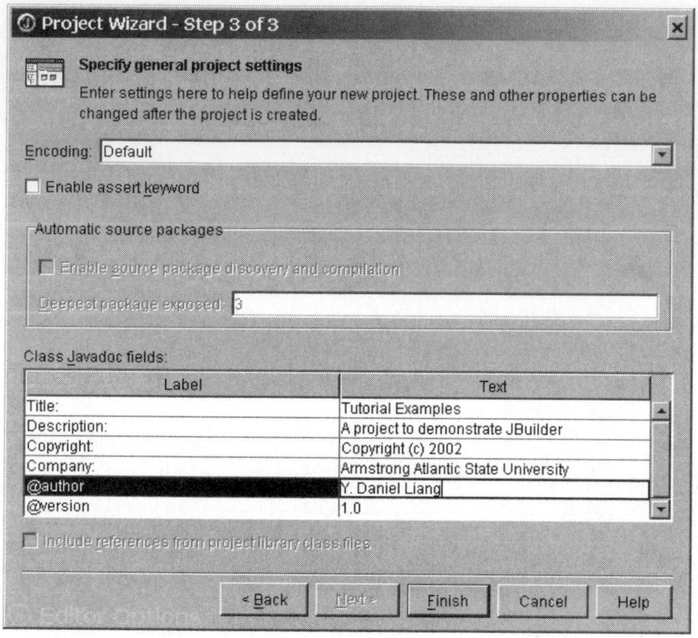

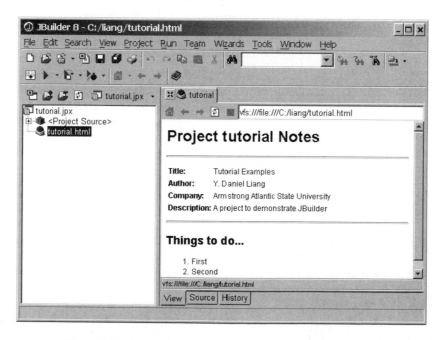

Figure 2.5   *Project Wizard—Step 3 of 3 collects optional information for the project.*

Figure 2.6   *A new project is created with the .jpx file and .html file.*

> *Caution*: Creating a project is a preliminary step before developing Java pro-
> grams. Creating projects incorrectly is a common problem for new JBuilder
> users, and can lead to frustrating mistakes. To avoid these, create your project
> exactly as shown in this section and change *liang* to your name.

2.2   Managing Projects in JBuilder (Optional)

JBuilder uses a project file to store project information. You cannot edit the project file
manually; it is modified automatically, however, whenever you add or remove files
from the project or set project properties. You can see the project file as a node at the
top of the project tree in the project pane (see Figure 2.6). JBuilder uses a Project
Properties dialog box for setting project properties and provides a Project wizard to fa-
cilitate creating projects.

> *Note*: The project properties can be modified in the Project Properties dialog
> box after a project file is created. However, there is no need to change any
> properties in order to use this book if you have set the path properties correct-
> ly in the Project wizard in JBuilder. That is why this section is marked optional.

2.2.1   Setting Project Properties

JBuilder uses the Default Project Properties dialog box to set default environment
properties for all projects. An individual project has its own Project Properties dialog
box, which can be used to set project-specific properties.

To display the Default Project Properties dialog box, select *Project, Default Properties*, as shown in Figure 2.7. To display the Project Properties dialog box, select *Project,
Properties*, as shown in Figure 2.8. You can also right-click the project file in the project
pane and choose the *Properties* command to display the Project Properties dialog box.

The Default Project Properties dialog box (Figure 2.7) and the Project Properties
dialog box (Figure 2.8) look the same but have different titles. Both dialog boxes contain Paths, General, Run, Build, Formatting, Class Filters, and Server. You can set options in these pages for the current project or the default project, depending on whether
the dialog box is for the current project or for the default project. JBuilder Personal and
JBuilder Standard have fewer options in the Project Properties dialog box.

2.2.2   The Paths Page

The Paths page of the Project Properties dialog box sets the following options:

- JDK version.
- Output path where the compilation output is stored.
- Backup path where the backup files are stored.
- Working directory where the temporary files are stored.
- Source page where the source files are stored.
- Documentation page where the Javadoc files are stored.
- Required Libraries page where the libraries are searched for compiling and running.

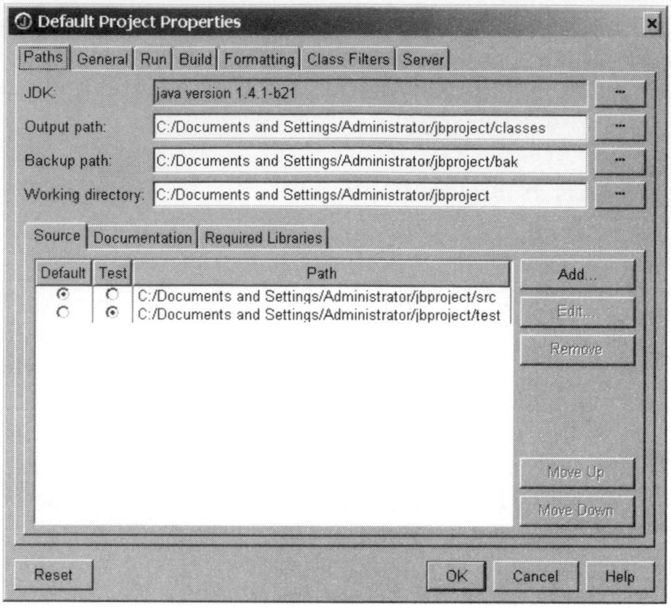

Figure 2.7   *The Default Project Properties dialog box enables you to set default properties to cover all your projects.*

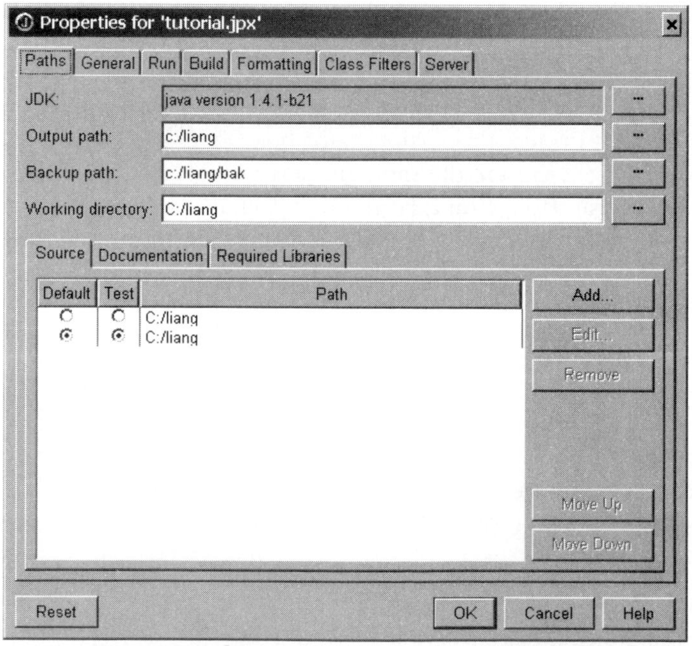

Figure 2.8   *Each project keeps its own project properties.*

JBuilder can compile and run against JDK 1.2, JDK 1.3, or JDK 1.4. To set up the list of available JDKs, click the Ellipsis button to display the Available JDK Versions dialog box for adding new JDK compilers. This feature is available only in JBuilder 8 Standard and Enterprise.

Setting proper paths is necessary for JBuilder to locate the associated files in the right directory for compiling and running the programs in the project. The Source page specifies one or more paths for the source file. The Output path specifies the path where the compiler places the .class files. Files are placed in a directory tree that is based on the Output path and the package name. For example, if the Output path is **c:\liang** and the package name is **tutorial** in the source code, the .class file is placed in **c:\liang\tutorial**. The Backup path specifies a directory where the backup source files are stored. JBuilder automatically backs up the files before committing any change to the current file. Note that the .java files are backed up in the backup directory, but the other files, like .html and .jpx, are backed up in their original directory. All the standard JDK libraries are already preinstalled. If you need to add the custom libraries to the project, click the *Add* button to display a list of available libraries. To remove a library, click the *Remove* button. To switch the order of libraries, use the *Move Up* and *Move Down* buttons.

2.2.3   The General Page

The General page (Figure 2.9) allows you to specify an encoding scheme used in JBuilder, enable or disable automatic source package discovery, and modify javadoc fields.

The "Encoding" choice menu specifies the encoding that controls how the compiler interprets characters beyond the ASCII character set. If no setting is specified, the default native-encoding converter for the platform is used. You can enable or disable the automatic source package. This is a useful feature available only in JBuilder Standard and Enterprise. With automatic source package enabled, all the packages in the project's source path automatically appear in the project pane, so you can navigate through the files without switching projects.

The Class Javadoc fields section specifies the javadoc tags generated in the class files when Generate Header Comments is enabled in a wizard.

2.2.4   The Run and Build Pages

The *Run* page displays runtime configurations. You can set new configurations. Using the preset parameters saves you time when running, debugging, and optimizing.

The *Build* page (Figure 2.10) has the *Java*, *General*, *IDL*, *Resource*, *Ant*, *Menu Items*, and *Web Services* tabs. The *Java* tab sets compiler options. You can choose a compiler, debug information, and target VM. The option "Show warnings" displays compiler warning messages. The option "Show deprecations" displays all deprecated classes, methods, properties, events, and variables used in the API. The option "Synchronize output dir" deletes class files on the output path for which you do not have source files before compiling. The option "Enable assert keyword" enables JDK 1.4 keyword `assert`. You need to check this option if your program uses assertions. The option "Obfuscate" makes your programs less vulnerable to decompiling. Decompiling means to translate the Java bytecode to Java source code. After decompiling your obfuscated

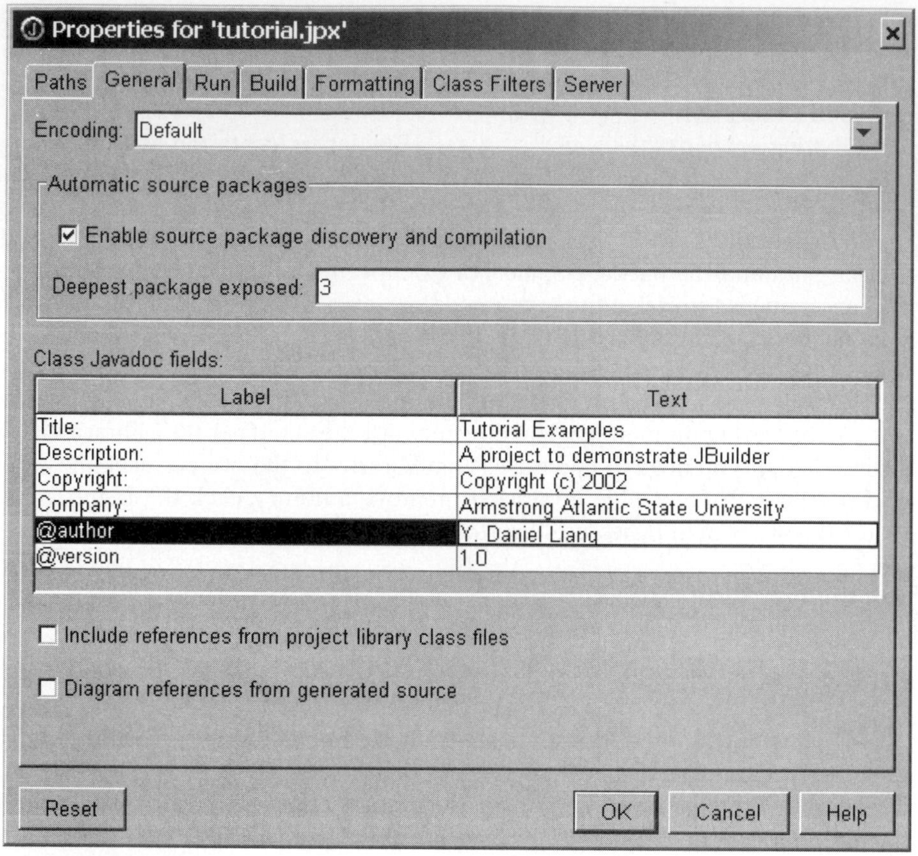

Figure 2.9 *The General page has options for selecting encoding type, enabling/disabling automatic source package discovery, and modifying javadoc fields.*

code, the generated source code contains altered symbol names for private symbols. This feature is available only in JBuilder Professional and Enterprise.

The *General* tab (Figure 2.11) lets you specify several build options. The option "Autosave all files before compiling" automatically saves all the files in the project before each compile. The option "Refresh project before building" refreshes the project pane before every build. The option "Generate source to output path" is applicable only to RMI (Remote Method Invocation) and IDL (Interface Definition Language) files. These files are used in multi-tier Java applications.

2.2.5 The Formatting Page

The *Formatting* page (Figure 2.12) enables you to specify how to format the code.

The *Basic* tab contains the options to control general indentation, tab size, and end-of-line characters. The *Blocks* tab controls different aspects of formatting for various

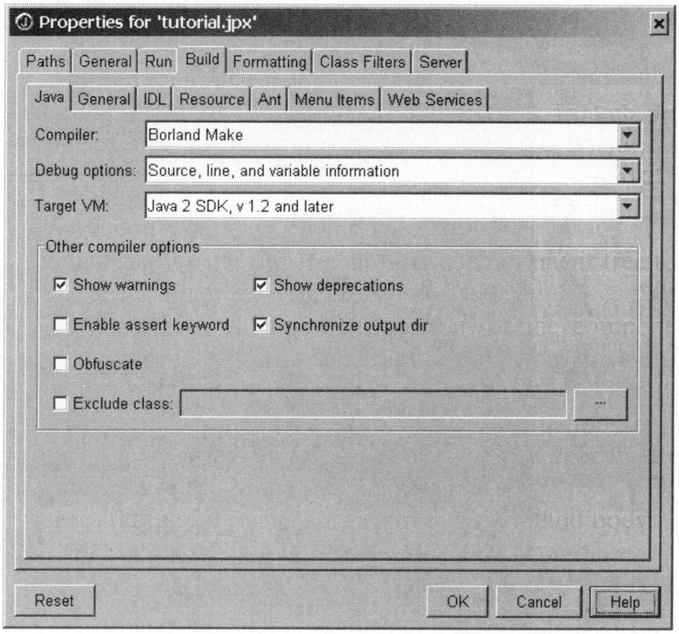

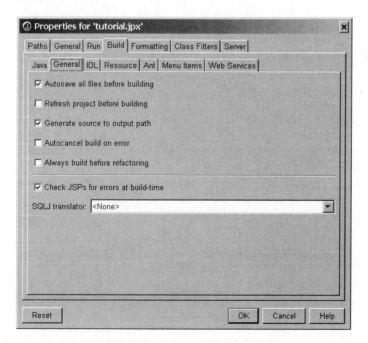

Figure 2.10   *The Build page sets compiler options.*

Figure 2.11   *The General tab sets build options.*

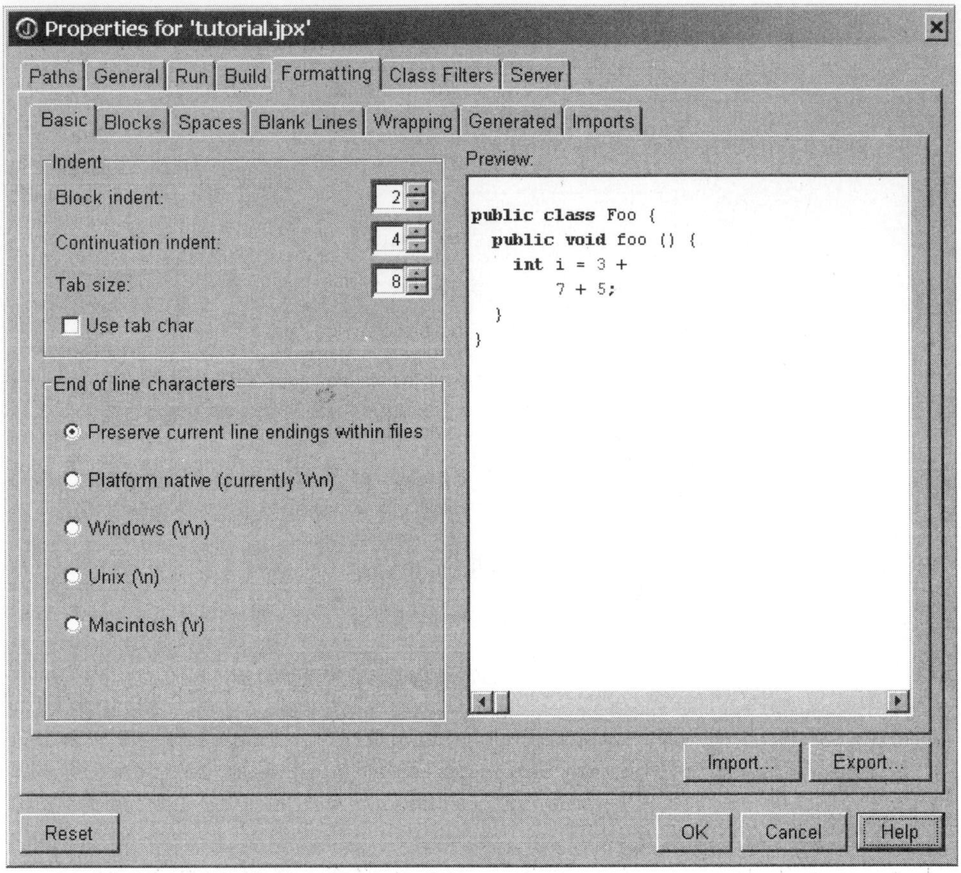

Figure 2.12 *The Formatting page of the Project Properties dialog box sets the options for formatting the code.*

types of code blocks. The *Spaces* tab enables you to specify where to insert space in your code to make the elements easier to see. The *Blank Lines* tab contains the options to control where blank lines are inserted in your code. The *Wrapping* tab controls where blank lines are inserted in your code. The *Generated* tab contains the options that tell JBuilder to generate event-handling code using an anonymous adapter or a standard adapter, or to match the existing style of event-handling code. The *Imports* tab controls how packages and files are imported into and displayed in the import statements section.

C H A P T E R   3

Creating, Compiling, and Running Java Programs

This chapter shows you how to create, compile, and run a Java program in JBuilder.

3.1 Creating a Java Program

There are many ways to create a Java program in JBuilder. This tutorial will show you how to use various wizards to create certain types of Java programs. In this section, you will learn how to create Java programs using the Class wizard.

The following are the steps in creating a Java program:

1. Open the tutorial.jpx project if it is not in the project pane. To open it, choose *File*, *Reopen* to display a submenu consisting of the most recently opened projects and files, as shown in Figure 3.1. Select the project if it is in the menu. Otherwise, choose *File*, *Open Project* to locate and open tutorial.jpx. The project file is the one with the (🔳) icon.

2. Choose *File*, *New Class* to display the Class wizard, as shown in Figure 3.2.

3. In the Class wizard, type `tutorial` in the Package field and `Welcome` in the Class name field, and check the options Public, Generate main method, and Generate header comments in the Options section, as shown in Figure 3.2. Click *OK* to generate Welcome.java, as shown in Figure 3.3.

4. Add the following line in the main method:
   ```
   System.out.println("Welcome to Java");
   ```

5. Select *File*, *Save All* to save all your work. You should see a confirmation message in the status bar indicating that the files are saved.

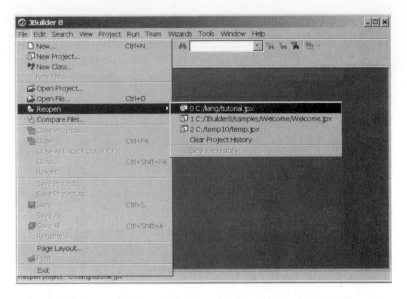

Figure 3.1   *Recently used projects can be reopened by choosing File, Reopen.*

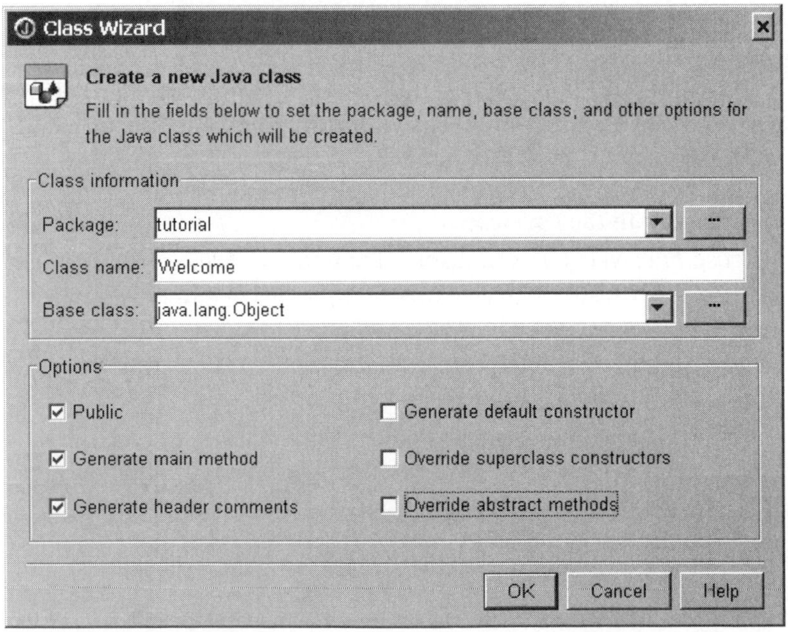

Figure 3.2   *You can use the Class wizard to create a template for a new class.*

```
JBuilder 8 - C:/liang/tutorial/Welcome.java                    _ □ ×
File  Edit  Search  View  Project  Run  Team  Wizards  Tools  Window  Help
```

```
tutorial.jpx
  <Project Source>
  tutorial
  tutorial.html
  Welcome.java

  Imports
  Welcome
      Welcome()
      main(String[] args)
```

```
  ×   tutorial   ×   Welcome
 1 package tutorial;
 2
 3 /**
 4  * <p>Title: </p>
 5  * <p>Description: </p>
 6  * <p>Copyright: Copyright (c) 2002</p>
 7  * <p>Company: </p>
 8  * @author not attributable
 9  * @version 1.0
10  */
11
12 public class Welcome {
13   public static void main(String[] args) {
14   }
15 }
```

```
Welcome.java                    Modified    Insert    1:1
Source  Design  Bean  UML  Doc  History
```

Figure 3.3   *The program Welcome.java is generated by the Class wizard.*

Note: As you type, the code completion assistance may automatically come up to give you suggestions for completing the code. For instance, when you type a dot (.) after **System** and pause for a second, JBuilder displays a popup menu with suggestions for completing the code, as shown in Figure 3.4. You can then select from the menu to complete the code.

Caution: Java source programs are case-sensitive. It would be wrong, for example, to replace **main** in the program with **Main**. Program file names are case-sensitive on UNIX and generally not case-sensitive on PCs, but file names are case-sensitive in JBuilder.

Tip: The public class name must match the file name. To change the file name, right-click the file in the project pane to display the context menu. Choose *Rename* in the context menu to change the file name, as shown in Figure 3.5. You can also delete the file from the context menu.

Note: You could type any package name (e.g., com.yourcompany.hostname) in the Package field in Figure 3.2. If you don't use the package statement in the program, leave the Package file blank in Figure 3.2.

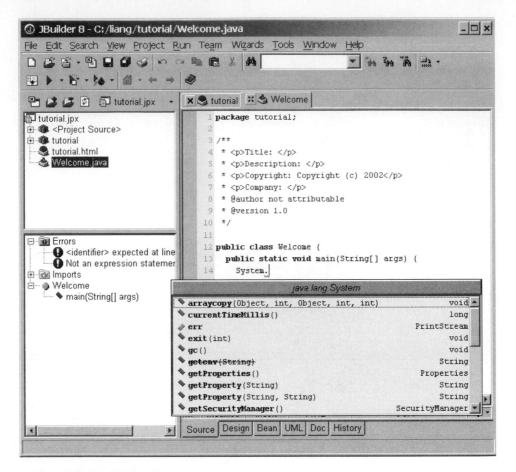

Figure 3.4   *The Code Insight popup menu is automatically displayed to help you complete the code.*

3.2   Compiling a Java Program

To compile **Welcome.java**, use one of the following methods. (Be sure that **Welcome.java** is selected in the project pane.)

- Choose *Project*, *Make "Welcome.java"* from the menu bar.
- Click the Make toolbar button (▣).
- Point to Welcome.java in the project pane, right-click the mouse button to display a popup menu (see Figure 3.5), and choose Make from the menu. (I find this method most useful.)

The compilation status is displayed on the status bar. If there are no syntax errors, the *compiler* generates a file named **Welcome.class**. This file is not an object file as generated

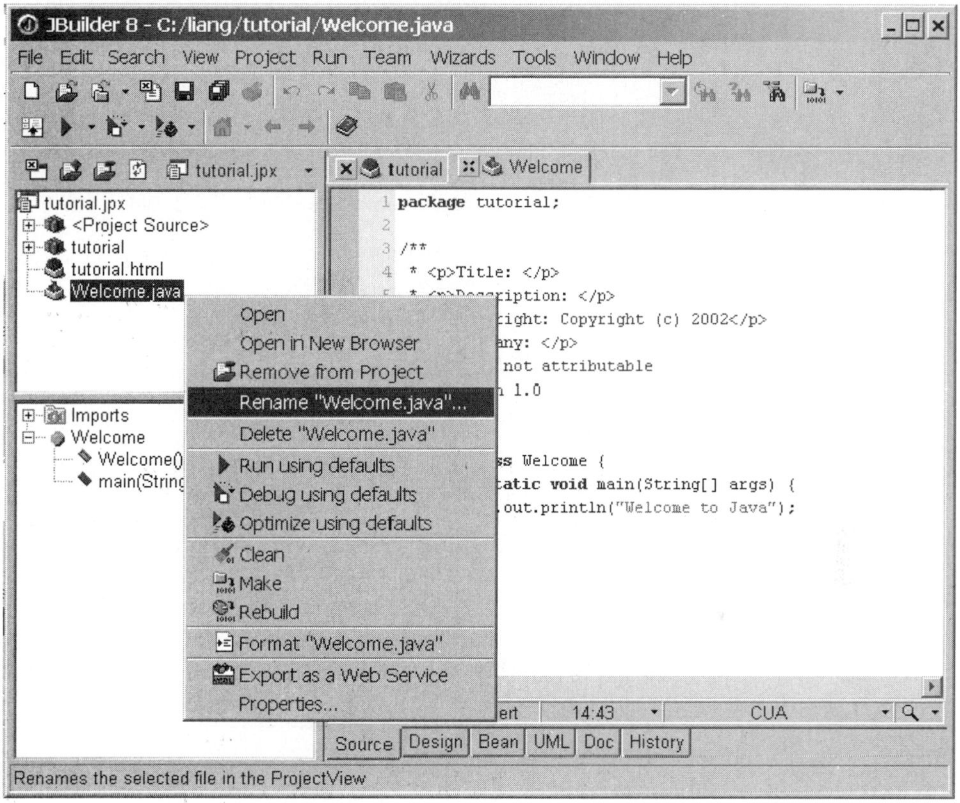

Figure 3.5 *The context menu of the file in the project pane has many useful commands.*

by other high-level language compilers. This file is called the *bytecode*. The bytecode is similar to machine instructions, but is architecture-neutral and can run on any platform that has the Java interpreter. This is one of Java's primary advantages: Java bytecode can run on a variety of hardware platforms and operating systems.

Note: The bytecode is stored in OutputPath\PackageName. Therefore, Welcome.class is stored in **c:\liang\tutorial**, since the Output path is set to **c:\liang** (see Figure 3.2) and the package name is **tutorial**. The file structures for the examples in this book are shown in Figure 3.6.

Tip: You can delete the .class file by choosing the *Clean* command from the context menu of the .java file in the project pane. You can delete all .class files in the project by choosing the *Clean* command from the context menu of the project node in the project pane.

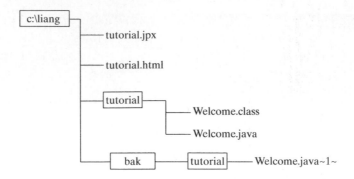

Figure 3.6   *Welcome.java and Welcome.class are placed in c:\liang\tutorial.*

Tip: The public class name must match the file name. To change the file name, right-click the file in the project pane to display the context menu. Choose *Rename* in the context menu to change the file name, as shown in Figure 3.5. You can also delete the file from the context menu.

Tip: As you type, the source code in the editor is dynamically parsed. The errors are displayed in the structure pane as shown in Figure 3.7.

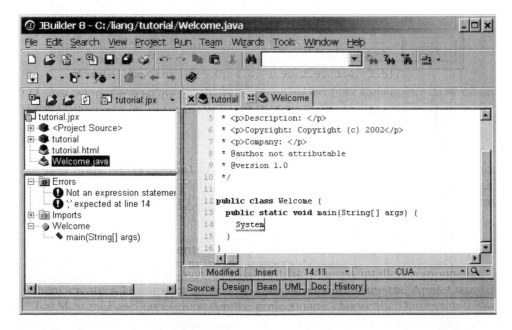

Figure 3.7   *JBuilder dynamically parses the source code and displays the syntax errors in the structure pane.*

3.3 Executing a Java Application

To run Welcome.class, point to Welcome.java in the project pane and right-click the mouse button to display a popup menu. Choose *Run Using Defaults* from the popup menu.

> *Note*: The Run command invokes the Compile command if the program is not compiled or was modified after the last compilation.

> *Note*: You could run a program by Choosing *Run*, *Run "Welcome.java"* from the main menu, or by clicking the Run toolbar button (▶), but then you have to specify a main class in the Runtime Properties dialog box. So it is more convenient to run a program from the project pane.

When this program executes, JBuilder displays the output in the message pane, as shown in Figure 3.8. The execution status is displayed below the message pane.

> *Tip*: If the message pane is not displayed, choose *View*, *Messages* to display it.

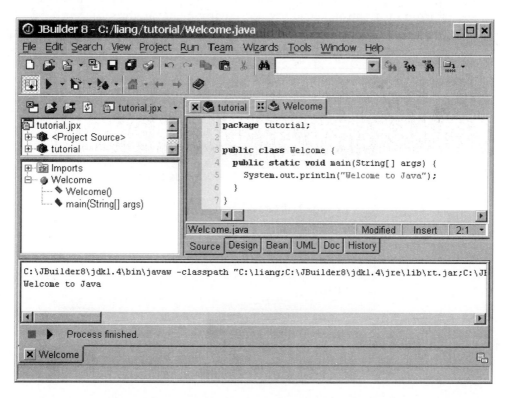

Figure 3.8 *The execution result is shown in the message pane.*

3.4   Run Java Applications from the Command Window

So far you have run programs in JBuilder IDE. You also can run program standalone directly from the operating system. Here are the steps in running the **Welcome** application from the DOS prompt.

1. Start a DOS window by clicking the Window's Start button, Programs, MS-DOS Prompt in Windows.
2. Type the following commands to set up proper environment variables for running Java programs in the DOS environment in Windows:

   ```
   set path=%path%;c:\JBuilder8\jdk1.4\bin
   set classpath=.;%classpath%
   ```

3. Type **cd c:\liang** to change the directory to **c:\liang**.
4. Type **java tutorial.Welcome** to run the program. A sample run of the output is shown in Figure 3.9.
   Insert the following two lines

   ```
   set path=%path%;c:\jBuilder8\jdk1.4\bin
   set classpath=.;%classpath%
   ```

in the autoexec.bat file on Windows 95 or Windows 98 to avoid setting the environment variables in Step 2 for every DOS session. On Windows NT or Windows 2000, select System from the Control Panel to set the environment variables.

Setting environment variables enables you to use the JDK command-line utilities. The java command invokes the Java interpreter to run the Java bytecode.

> *Note*: You can also compile the program using the javac command at the DOS prompt, as shown in Figure 3.9.

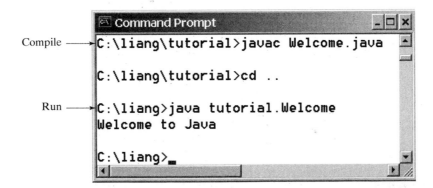

Compile
```
C:\liang\tutorial>javac Welcome.java

C:\liang\tutorial>cd ..
```
Run
```
C:\liang>java tutorial.Welcome
Welcome to Java

C:\liang>_
```

Figure 3.9   *You can run a Java program from the DOS prompt using the java command.*

CHAPTER 4

Creating and Testing Java Applets

You have learned how to create, compile, and execute a Java program. Applets are special type of Java program. JBuilder provides the Applet wizard that can be used to create Java applets.

4.1   Creating a Java Applet

The following steps create template files for a new applet:

1. Choose *File*, *New* to display the object gallery, as shown in Figure 4.1. In the Web page of the Object Gallery, click the Applet icon to open the Applet wizard.
2. JBuilder starts Applet Wizard-Step 1 of 4 to configure your applet (see Figure 4.2). Edit the Package field to `tutorial` and the Class field to `WelcomeApplet`, choose `javax.swing.JApplet` in the Base class field, and check the *Generate header comments* and *Can run standalone* options, as shown in Figure 4.2. Click *Finish* to generate the template files for the applet.

> *Note*: You may choose the *Next* button to display Step 2 of 4 of the Applet wizard to enter the parameters for the applet.

The Applet wizard generates two files: WelcomeApplet.html and WelcomeApplet.java. The source code for WelcomeApplet.html is shown in the content pane of the AppBrowser in Figure 4.3. The source code for WelcomeApplet.java is shown in Figure 4.4.

> *Note*: The HTML file WelcomeApplet.html is stored in the project source path directory (e.g., **c:\liang**) and the Java source file WelcomeApplet.java is stored in the project source path directory/package Name (e.g., **c:\liang\tutorial**). To view the code in WelcomeApplet.html, you need to choose the Source tab at the bottom of the content pane.

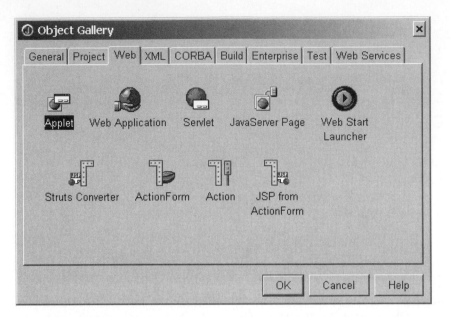

Figure 4.1 *The object gallery contains many useful wizards for creating various types of Java programs.*

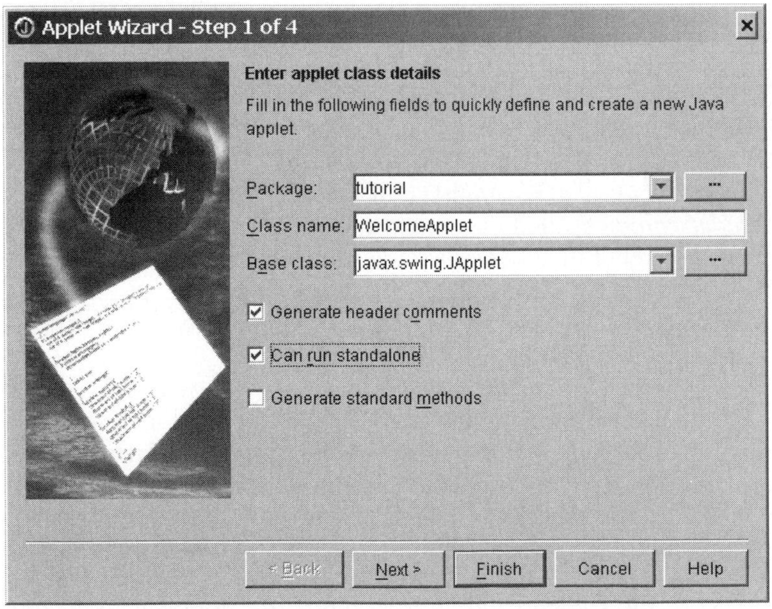

Figure 4.2 *Applet Wizard-Step 1 of 3 prompts you to enter the package name, the applet class name, and other optional information.*

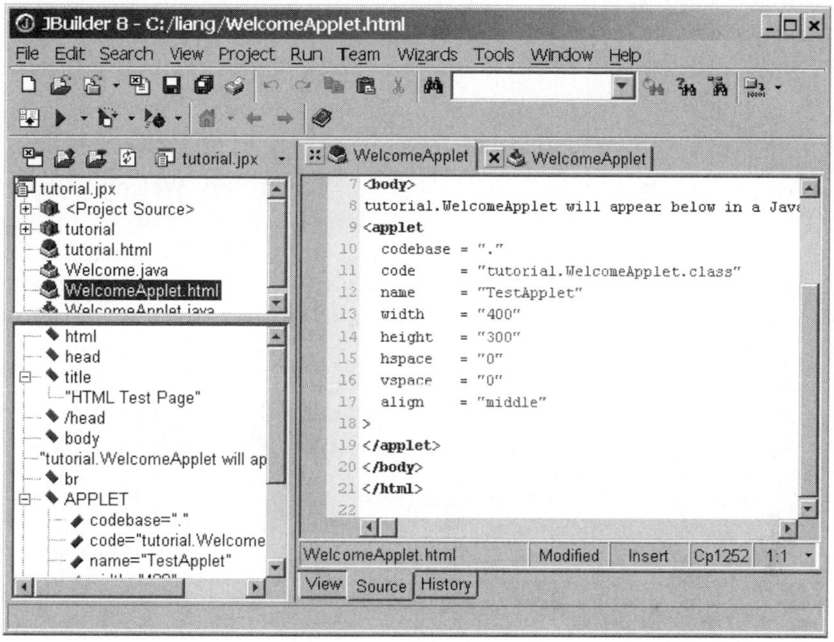

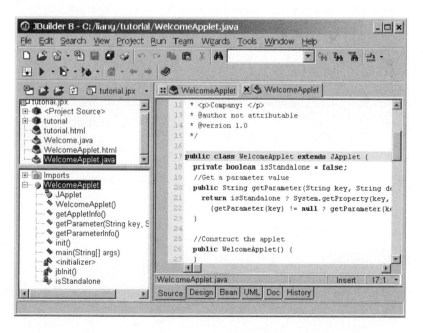

Figure 4.3   *The source code of WelcomeApplet.html is shown in the content pane.*

Figure 4.4   *The source code of WelcomeApplet.java is shown in the content pane.*

4.2 Modifying Applets

The Applet wizard generates a template for the applet class that contains six methods: `getAppletInfo`, `getParameter`, `getParameterInfo`, `init`, `jbInit`, and `main`. The `main` method is generated because you checked *Can run standard alone* option in Figure 4.2. The methods `getAppletInfo`, `getParameterInfo`, and `init` are defined in the `java.applet.Applet` class and are overridden in WelcomeApplet.java. The `getParameter` method in `WelcomeApplet` has the same name as the `getParameter` method in the `Applet` class. The two methods have different signatures, however. The `getParameter` method in `WelcomeApplet` returns a default value if the parameter does not exist in the HTML file. The `jbInit` method initializes the applet user interface; it is called by the `init` method. You should add the code in the `jbInit` method to create the user interface.

Add the following line in the `jbInit` method to display the text "Welcome to Java" in the label and place the label in the center of the applet.

```
getContentPane().add(new JLabel("Welcome to Java", JLabel.CENTER));
```

When you run the program, you will see the text displayed in the applet.

4.3 Viewing Applets in the Content Pane

You can view the applet in the content pane using the JBuilder's applet viewer by selecting the applet's HTML file (e.g., WelcomeApplet.html) in the project pane and choosing the View tab in the content pane, as shown in Figure 4.5.

Figure 4.5 *The applet is displayed in the content pane inside JBuilder IDE.*

4.4 Viewing Applets Using the Applet Viewer Utility

You can also view a Java applet using the Sun applet viewer. Choose the applet's HTML file (e.g., WelcomeApplet.html) in the project pane. Right-click it to display its context menu. Click *Run using defaults* in the context menu. The applet is displayed in the applet viewer, as shown in Figure 4.6.

You can also invoke the applet viewer from the DOS prompt using the following command:

```
appletviewer WelcomeApplet.html
```

Figure 4.6   *The WelcomeApplet program is running from the applet viewer.*

4.5 Viewing Applets from a Web Browser

Applets are eventually displayed in a Web browser. Using JBuilder's applet viewer and Sun's applet viewer, you do not need to start a Web browser. Both applet viewers function as browsers. They are convenient for testing applets before deploying them on a Web site. JBuilder's applet viewer has limited functions. For example, you cannot use menus from JBuilder's applet viewer. Sun's applet viewer fully simulates a Web browser. To display an applet from a Web browser, open the applet's HTML file (e.g., WelcomeApplet.html). Its output is shown in Figure 4.7.

Figure 4.7   *The WelcomeApplet program is displayed in Internet Explorer 6.*

Note: You have to view the applet in Figure 4.7 using a Web browser that supports Java 2. At present, Netscape 6/7 and IE 6 support Java 2. To view the applets from other browsers, such as IE 5.0 and Netscape 4.7, you have to use the Java Plug-In. Please see supplements for information on Java Plug-In, at *www.cs.armstrong.edu/liang/jbtutorial.html*.

To make your applet accessible on the Web, you need to store the WelcomeApplet.class and WelcomeApplet.html on a Web server. You can view the applet from an appropriate URL. For example, I have uploaded these two files on Web server *www.cs.armstrong.edu*. As shown in Figure 4.8, you can access the applet from *www.cs.armstrong.edu/liang/jbtutorial/WelcomeApplet.html*.

Figure 4.8   *The WelcomeApplet program is downloaded from the Web server.*

C H A P T E R   5

JBuilder's Online Help

JBuilder provides a large number of documents online, giving you a great deal of information on a variety of topics pertaining to the use of JBuilder and Java.

5.1 Accessing from the Help Menu

To access online help, choose *Help*, *Help Topics* to display JBuilder Help, as shown in Figure 5.1.

JBuilder Help behaves like a Web browser and contains the main menus, navigation pane, and content pane. From the main menus, you can open a URL from the File

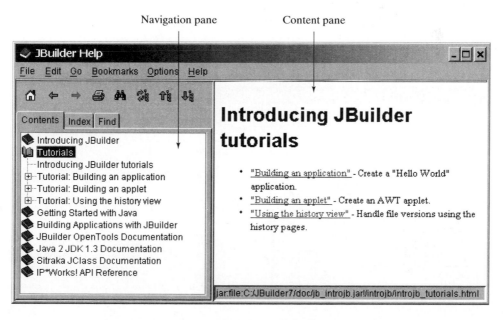

Figure 5.1 *All help documents are displayed in JBuilder Help.*

menu, add bookmarks from the Bookmarks menu, and get help on using JBuilder Help from the Help menu.

The navigation pane contains eight action buttons on top of the three tabs. The buttons are *Home, Previous, Next, Print, Find in Page, Synchronize Table of Contents, Previous Topics*, and *Next Topic*. The Home, Previous, and Next buttons let you go to the first, previous, and next topics in the history list. The Print button prints the document in the content pane. The Find in Page button enables you to search the current topic. The Synchronize Table of Contents button synchronizes the topic with the contents in the content pane. The Previous Topic and Next Topic buttons let you go to the previous and next topics.

The three tabs are *Contents, Index*, and *Find*. The Contents tab displays available documents. The table of contents of the document is displayed in a tree-like list in the navigation pane. To view a given topic, select the node in the tree associated with the topic. JBuilder Help displays the document for the topic in the content pane.

The Index tab shows the index entries for the current document. The Find page shows the combined index entries for all the available documents in JBuilder. To display the index, simply type the first few letters in the entry. As you start typing, the index scrolls, doing an incremental search on the index entries to find the closest match. Select and double-click the index in the entry to display the document for the entry in the content pane.

5.2   Obtaining Help on Java Keywords and Classes

To obtain help on a Java keyword, highlight it in the content pane and press F1. For example, if you highlight *public* in the content pane, as shown in Figure 5.2, and press F1, you will see the help on *public* displayed in Figure 5.3.

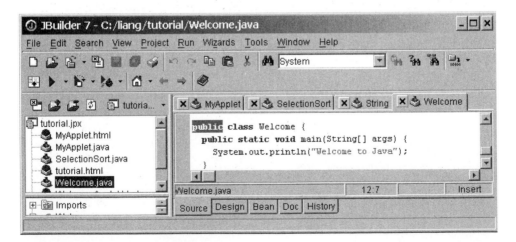

Figure 5.2   *Highlight* `public` *and press F1 to display the documentation on the keyword* `public`.

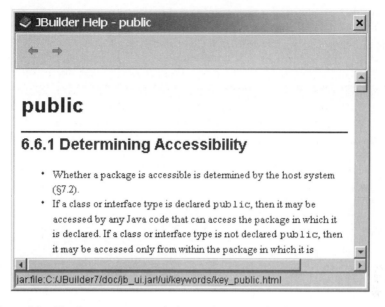

Figure 5.3   *The documentation on the keyword* `public` *is displayed in JBuilder Help.*

To display the documentation on a Java class, highlight the class name (e.g., *String*) in the content pane and press F1. The documentation for the class is displayed in JBuilder Help, as shown in Figure 5.4.

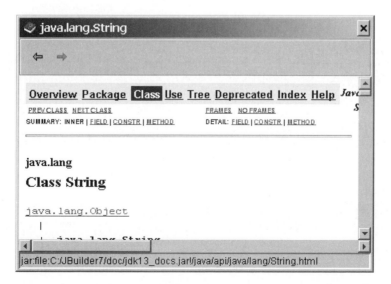

Figure 5.4   *The documentation on the* `String` *class is displayed in JBuilder Help.*

You can also display the source code of the class by choosing *Find Definition* in the context menu of the class in the content pane, as shown in Figure 5.5. The class source code is displayed in the content pane.

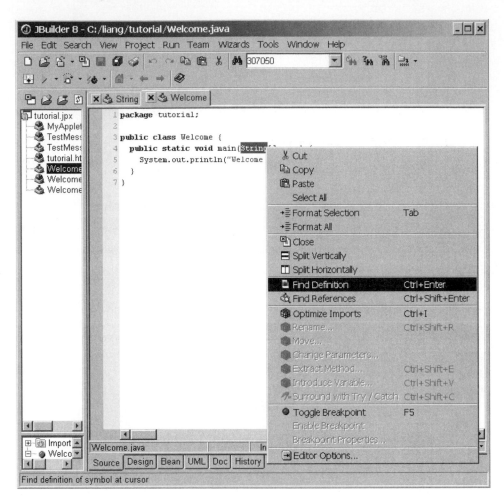

Figure 5.5   *The source code of the class is displayed in the content pane.*

CHAPTER 6

Customizing JBuilder Environment

JBuilder allows you to customize your development environment by changing the IDE options or the Editor options. Certain options, such as syntax highlighting, make your programs easy to read and help you to spot errors.

6.1 Setting IDE Options

To set the IDE options, choose *Tools*, *IDE Options* to display the IDE Options dialog box, as shown in Figure 6.1. The dialog box contains the tabs *Browser*, *File Types*, *Web*, *XML*, *Run/Debug*, *Audio*, *UML*, and *EJB Designer*.

6.1.1 The Browser Page

In the Browser tab, you can set the look-and-feel of the AppBrowser. Three types of look-and-feel (Metal, Motif, and Windows) are available in the Windows version of JBuilder. For example, if you choose Metal in the look-and-feel combo box, the IDE Options dialog would be displayed as shown in Figure 6.2.

In the IDE Options dialog box, you can also set the orientation of the tabs in the content pane and set the label type for the tabs in the content pane, as shown in Figure 6.3.

6.1.2 The File Types Page

In the File Types tab, you can set the options for file extensions for the types of files in the File Types tab. For example, you can add or remove a file extension, as shown in Figure 6.4.

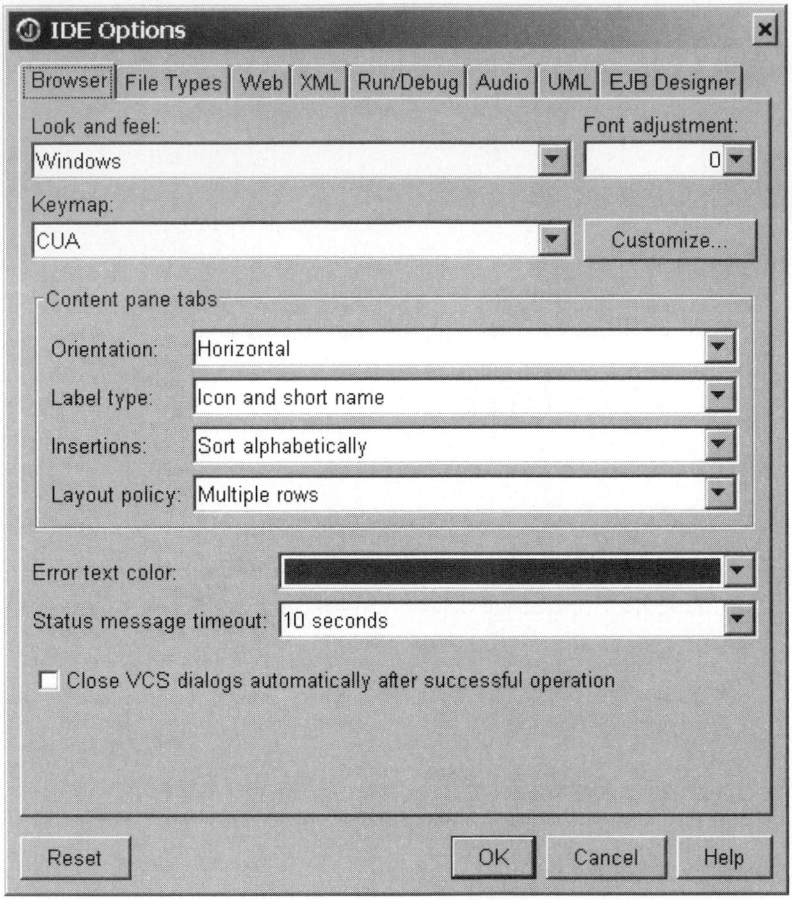

Figure 6.1   *The IDE Options dialog box enables you to set the options for the Browser, File Types, Run/Debug, and Audio.*

6.1.3   The Run/Debug Page

In the Run/Debug tab, you can set runtime update intervals and debugger update intervals, as shown in Figure 6.5. If these intervals are small, the debugger/runtime responses for output and other events, like stepping, will be faster, but JBuilder will be using most of the CPU time. In general, make these settings small unless you are running other applications along with JBuilder or the program you are debugging requires a lot of CPU time. If this is the case, make these intervals larger.

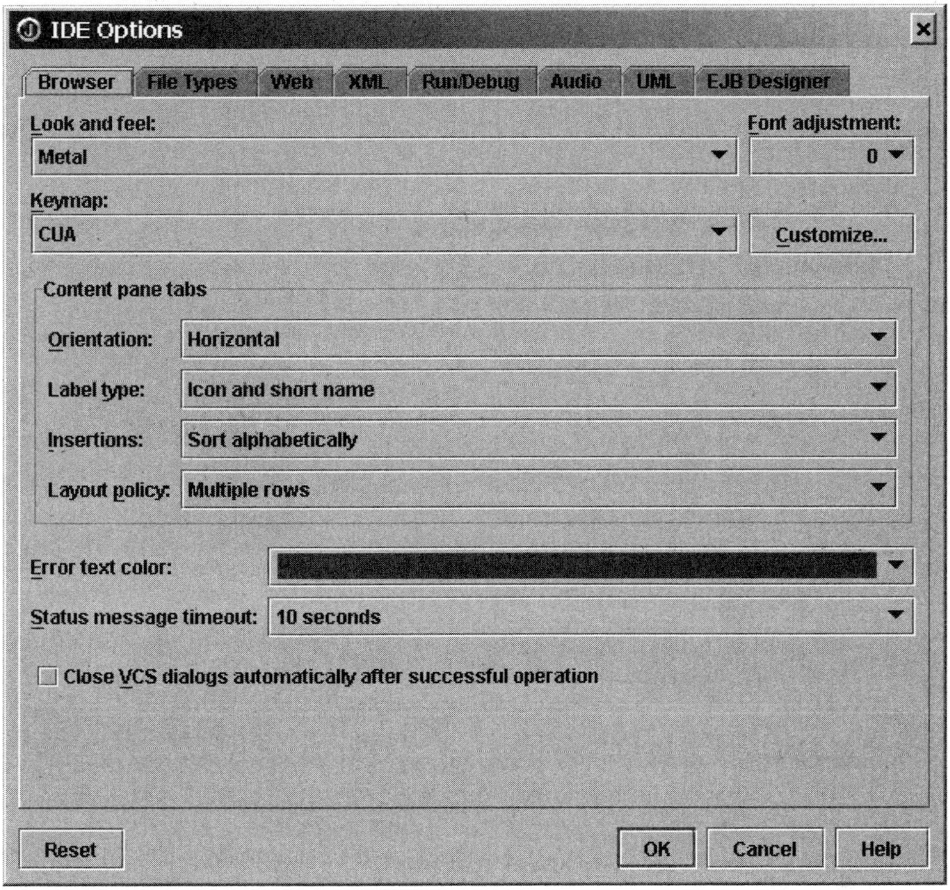

Figure 6.2   *The IDE Options dialog box appears in Metal look-and-feel.*

6.1.4   The Audio Page

You can enable or disable audio for various events in JBuilder, as shown in Figure 6.6. You can also adjust the volume of the audio. Audio is attached to various events and is enabled by default. JBuilder provides an audio theme stored in JBuilder's lib/audio/ directory. You can also add custom audio files and attach them to specified events.

6.2   Setting Editor Options

To set Editor options, choose *Tools, Editor Options* to display the Editor Options dialog box, as shown in Figure 6.7. The dialog box contains six tabs: *Editor, Display, Color, CodeInsight, Templates*, and *Java Structure*.

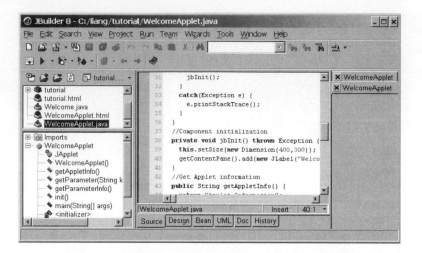

Figure 6.3   *The file tabs in the content pane are displayed vertically because of a change in the IDE option dialog box.*

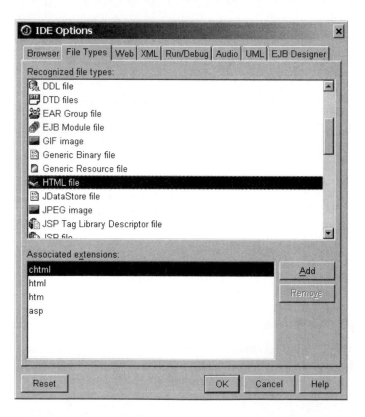

Figure 6.4   *You can set a file extension in the IDE Options dialog box.*

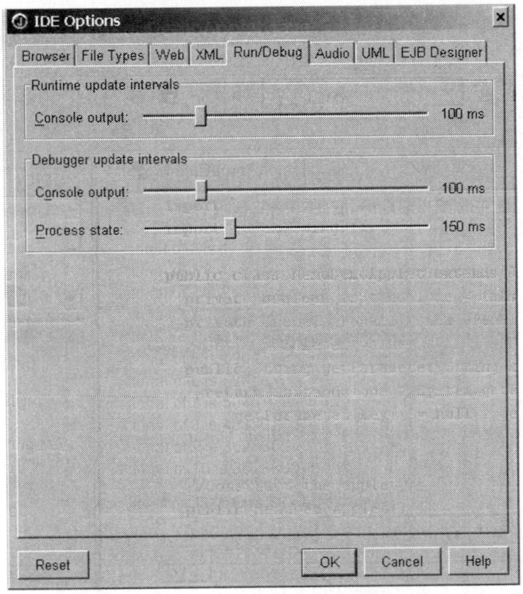

Figure 6.5 *You can set the options for runtime update intervals and debugger update intervals.*

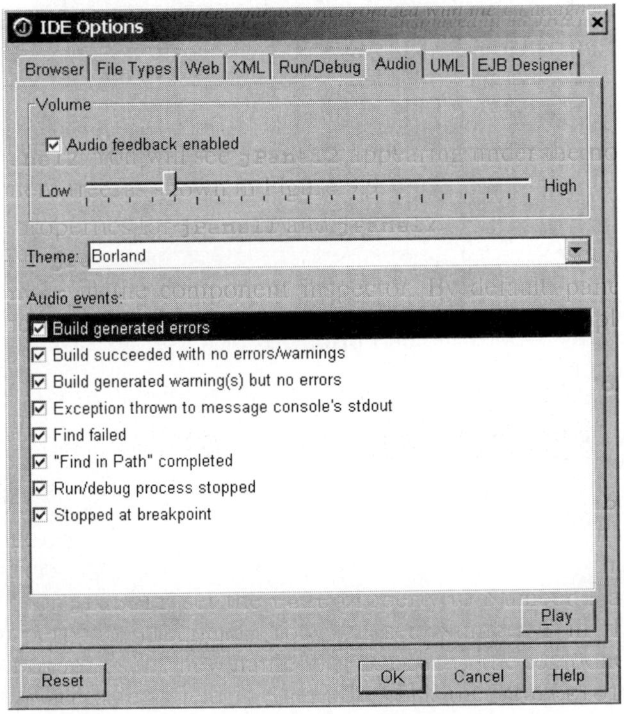

Figure 6.6 *You can set the options for audios in JBuilder.*

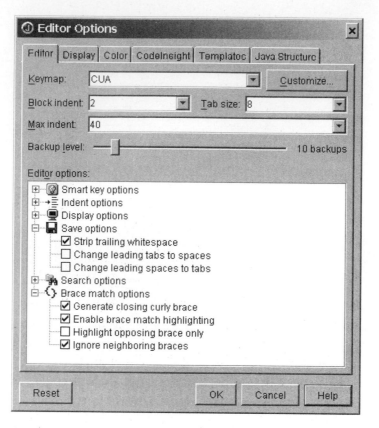

Figure 6.7   *The Editor Options dialog box enables you to set the options for editing in the content pane.*

6.2.1   The Editor Page

The Editor tab enables you to customize editing behavior in the content pane. You can set the smart key options, indent options, display options, save options, search options, and brace match options.

6.2.2   The Display Page

The Display tab (see Figure 6.8) enables you to set the right margin and the fonts for the content pane.

6.2.3   The Color Page

The Color tab (see Figure 6.9) specifies the colors of the different elements of your code in the source pane. You can specify foreground and background colors for the elements, such as Comment, Reserved word, String, Symbol, and Error line, in the Element list. The sample code at the bottom of the dialog box shows how your settings will appear in the source pane.

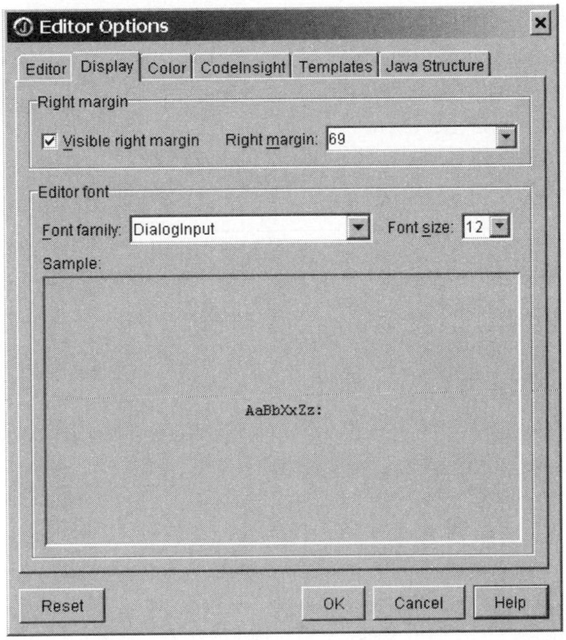

Figure 6.8 *You can customize display and font options for the content pane in the Display tab of the Editor Options dialog box.*

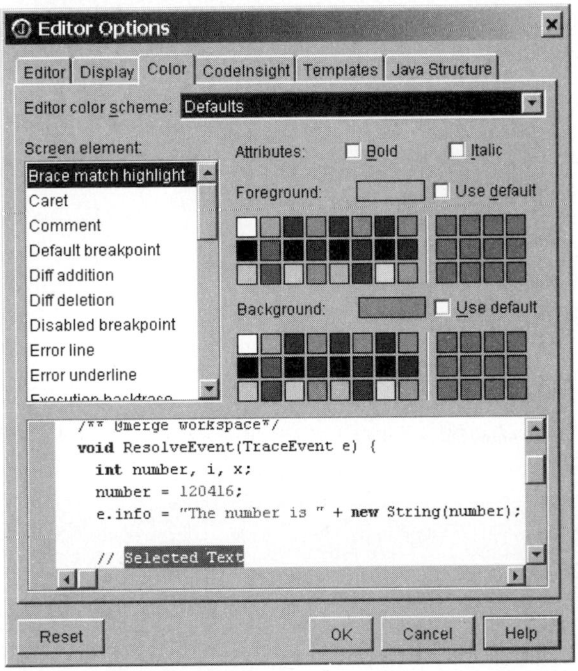

Figure 6.9 *You can customize colors for different elements of the source code.*

6.2.4   The CodeInsight Page

The CodeInsight tab (see Figure 6.10) enables you to configure Code Insight (Code completion assistant). JBuilder's Code Insight enhancements display a context-sensitive popup window within the Editor. Code Insight provides code completion, parameter lists, and tool tip expression evaluation. Code Insight highlights illegal class references not on the Class Path and invalid statements not found in the classes.

> *Tip*: If the cursor is between the parentheses for a method call, pressing Ctrl+Shift+H or Ctrl+Shift+Space brings up a list of valid parameters.

6.2.5   The Templates Page

The Templates tab (see Figure 6.11) displays JBuilder's predefined code templates. Code templates are snippets of frequently used code elements that you can insert into

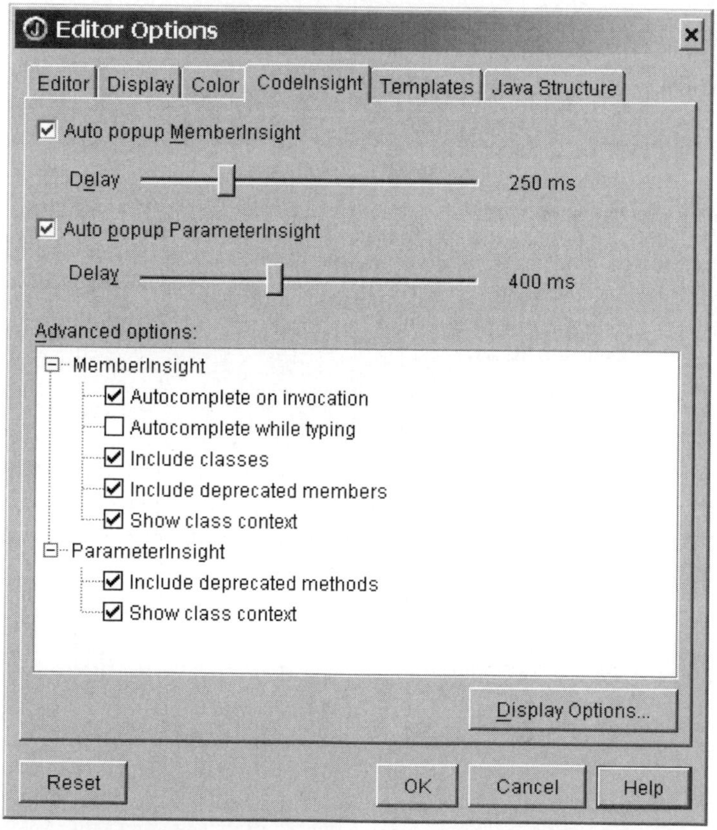

Figure 6.10   *You can specify whether and how to use Code Insight on the CodeInsight tab of the Editor Options dialog box.*

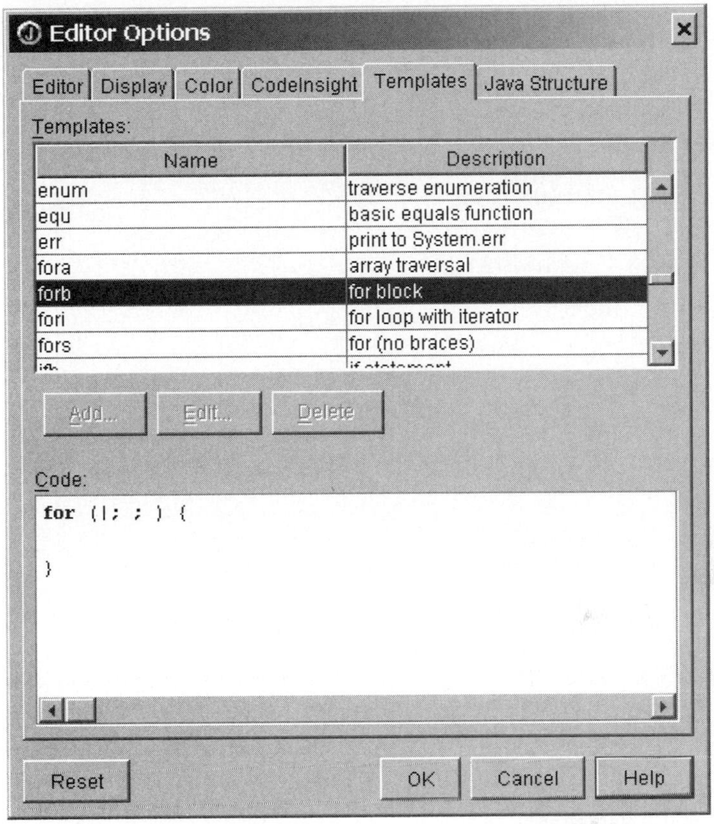

Figure 6.11 *You can add, edit, or delete code templates in the Templates tab.*

your code to avoid repetitive typing. To use code templates, choose one of the following two methods:

- Type the code template name, such as *forb*, in your code where you want the code to appear and press CTRL+J to generate the template for the **for** loop block.
- Position the cursor where you want the code to appear and press CTRL+J to display a list of template names. Select a template from the list. The template is automatically created.

6.2.6 The Java Structure Page

The Java Structure tab (see Figure 6.12) contains the options for specifying the appearance of the code elements in the structure pane.

> *Tip*: The Java Structure dialog box can also be displayed by right-clicking the mouse button in the structure pane to display a popup menu. The popup menu contains the item named Properties. Choose Properties to display the Java Structure View Properties dialog box, as shown in Figure 6.13.

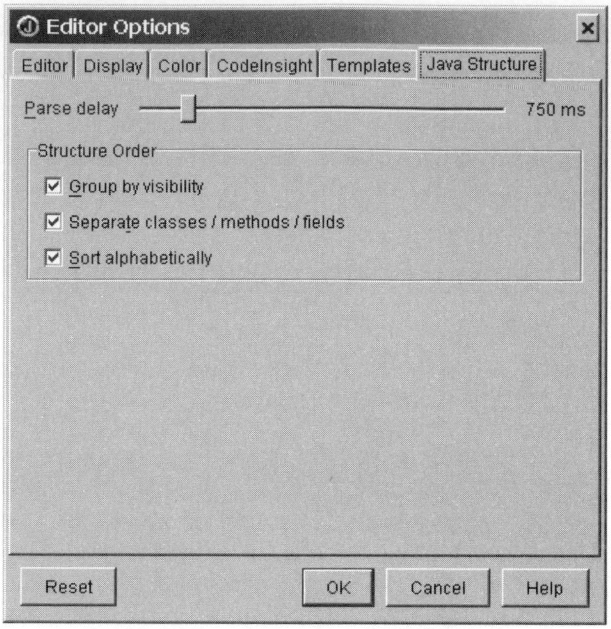

Figure 6.12 *The Java Structure tab enables you to specify the appearance of the code elements in the structure pane.*

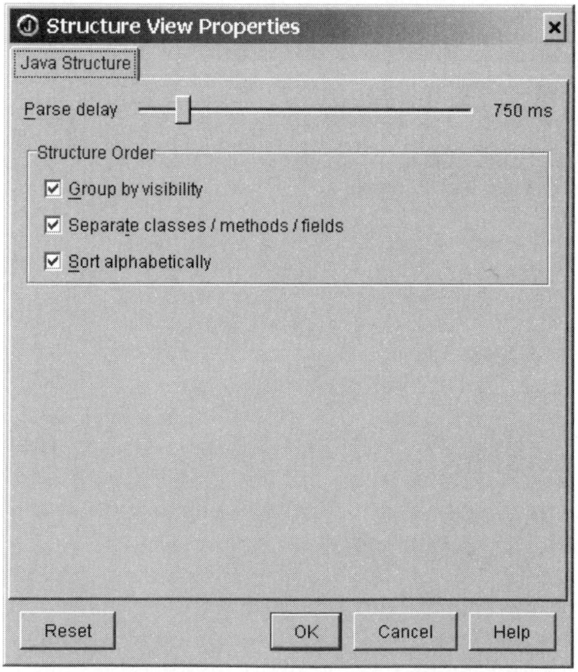

Figure 6.13 *The Structure View Properties dialog box can be displayed from the context menu in the structure pane.*

CHAPTER 7

JBuilder Menu Commands

The main menu contains commands similar to those of other Windows applications. This chapter introduces the commands in the File, Edit, Search, View, Project, and Run menus.

7.1   The File Commands

The *File* menu (see Figure 7.1) contains the commands for creating and opening projects, for creating, opening, saving, and closing files, for printing files, and for exiting JBuilder. The *Close Files* command enables you to close all the files in the content pane except the current file. The *Rename* command enables you to rename the file name that is currently displayed in the content pane.

> *Tip*: If the Print command is dimmed, click the content pane to activate it.

7.2   The Edit Commands

The *Edit* menu (see Figure 7.2) contains the standard Windows commands for editing text, such as *Undo*, *Redo*, *Cut*, *Copy*, *Paste*, and *Delete*. It also contains the *Format* command for formatting the source code, the commands for code insight, parameter insight, and class insight.

> *Tip*: To use the Format command, you need to highlight the code first, and then click the Format command.

7.3   The Search Commands

You can use the commands in the *Search* menu to find and/or replace text in source code, to search text in multiple files in the source paths, to position the cursor at a specific line, and to find classes. The Search menu is shown in Figure 7.3.

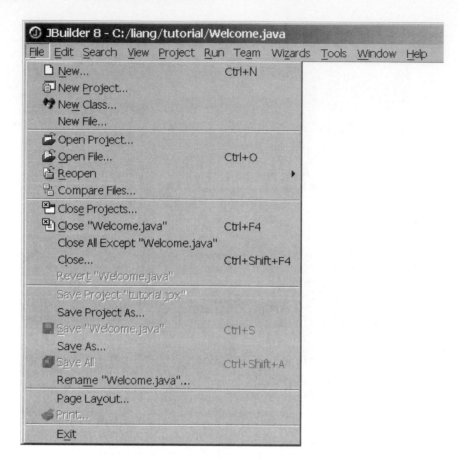

Figure 7.1   *The File menu contains commands for handling files and projects.*

In JBuilder 8, Find and Replace share the same dialog box. To find or replace text in the current content pane, choose either the Find command or the Replace command to display the Find/Replace Text dialog box, as shown in Figure 7.4. Use this dialog box to specify the text you want to locate, or replace. You can set options such as direction, scope, and origin, as well as case-sensitive and whole-word searches.

To replace text in the current content pane, type the replacement text in the Replace with field, and press the Replace button in the Find/Replace Text dialog box to display the Confirm replace dialog box, as shown in Figure 7.5. To replace all matching text, you can press the All button in this dialog box.

The *Search Again* command repeats the last search, replace, or incremental search.

The *Incremental Search* command moves the cursor directly to the next occurrence of text that you type. When you are performing an incremental search, the content pane status line reads "Searching For": and displays each letter you have typed. Press Enter or Escape to cancel incremental search.

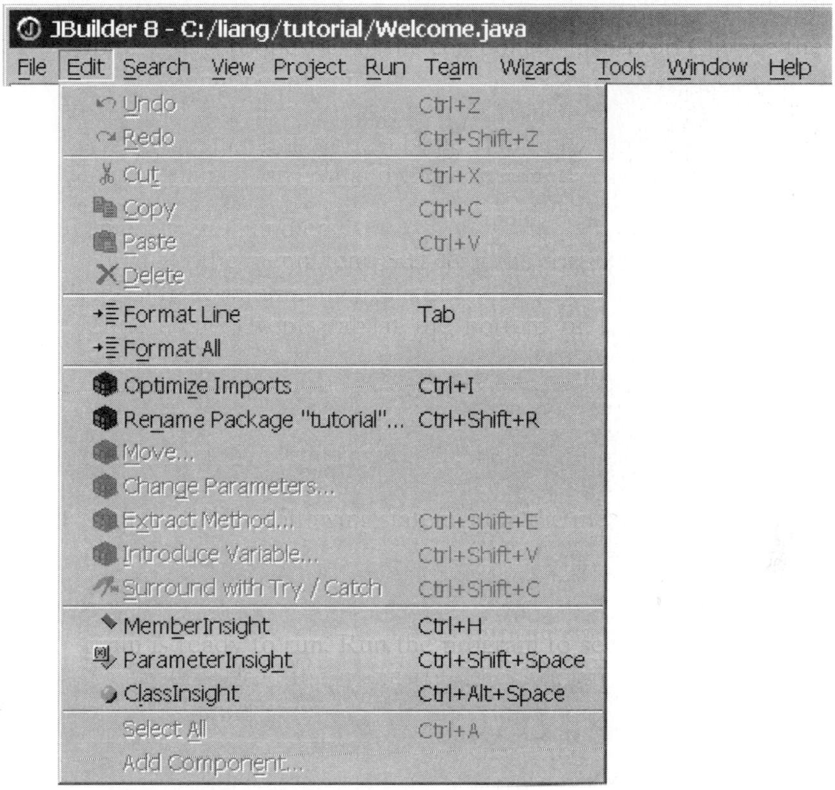

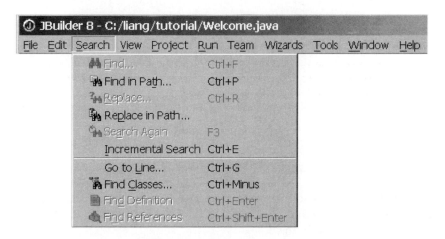

Figure 7.2 *The Editor menu contains commands for editing text.*

Figure 7.3 *The Search menu contains commands for searching and replacing text in the source file, and for browsing classes.*

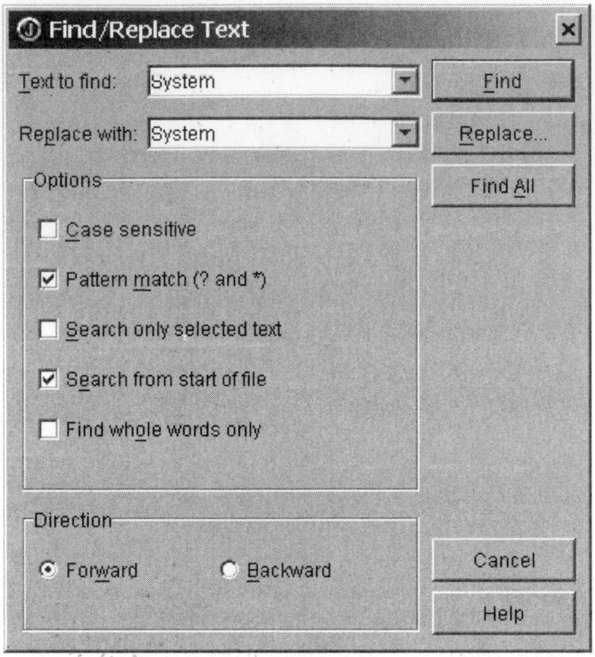

Figure 7.4   *The Find/Replace Text dialog box lets you search or replace a string.*

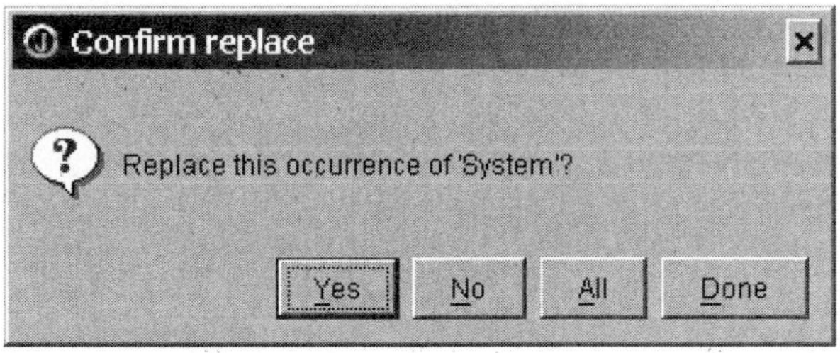

Figure 7.5   *The Confirm replace dialog box prompts you to specify whether to replace the text or how to replace the text.*

Occasionally, you want to search for text in multiple files. JBuilder enables you to use the *Find in Path* command to search for a string in all the .java files in the specified path, as shown in Figure 7.6.

The Go to Line command enables you to move the cursor directly to a specified line number, as shown in Figure 7.7.

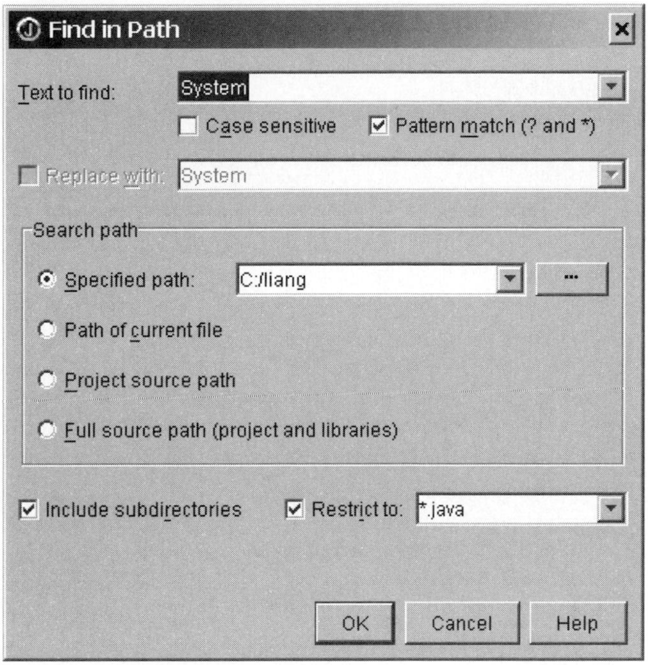

Figure 7.6   *The Find in Path dialog box lets you specify text to search for in all the files in the path.*

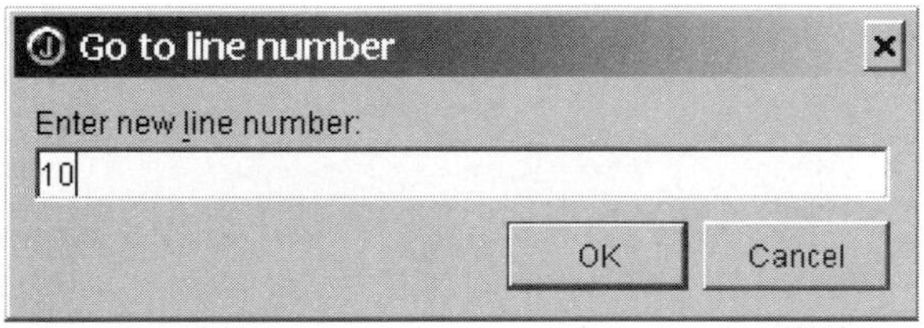

Figure 7.7   *You can move the cursor directly to the specified line number.*

The *Find Classes* command displays the Find Classes dialog box, as shown in Figure 7.8. Use this dialog box to view the source code and documentation of a class.

7.4   The View Commands

The View menu (see Figure 7.9) contains commands for displaying or hiding toolbar buttons, project pane, content pane, structure pane, message pane, and status bar.

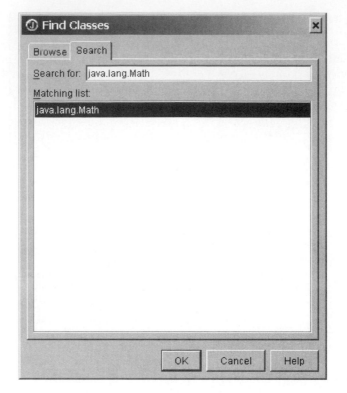

Figure 7.8 *The Find Classes dialog box lets you find a class and examine its contents.*

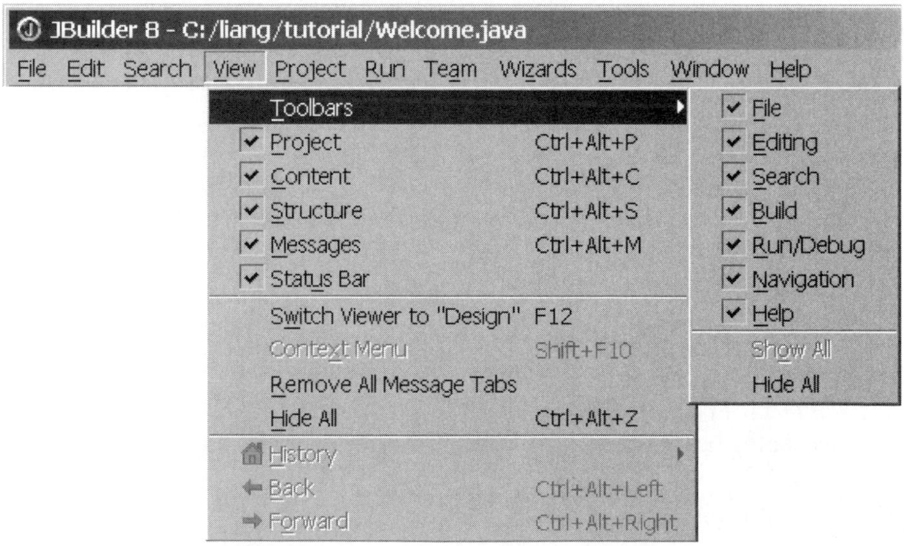

Figure 7.9 *The View menu controls the display of various panes in JBuilder.*

7.5   The Project Commands

The Project menu (see Figure 7.10) contains the commands for compiling the project, adding files, and displaying default or current project properties dialog boxes. The Make command compiles any .java files in the selected node that have outdated or nonexistent .class files. It also compiles any imported programs that have outdated or nonexistent .class files.

The selected node can be a project, package, or .java file. Making a package or project includes all the .java files in the package or project, including those in nested packages.

The imported files that are checked and compiled include all recursively imported files (i.e., imported files of imported files) except for files in stable packages that are not part of the project.

The Rebuild command compiles all .java files in the selected node, regardless of whether their .class files are outdated. It also compiles the imported files upon which the node depends, regardless of whether their .class files are outdated.

> *Tip*: Once you have done the initial compiling, Make is faster than Rebuild.

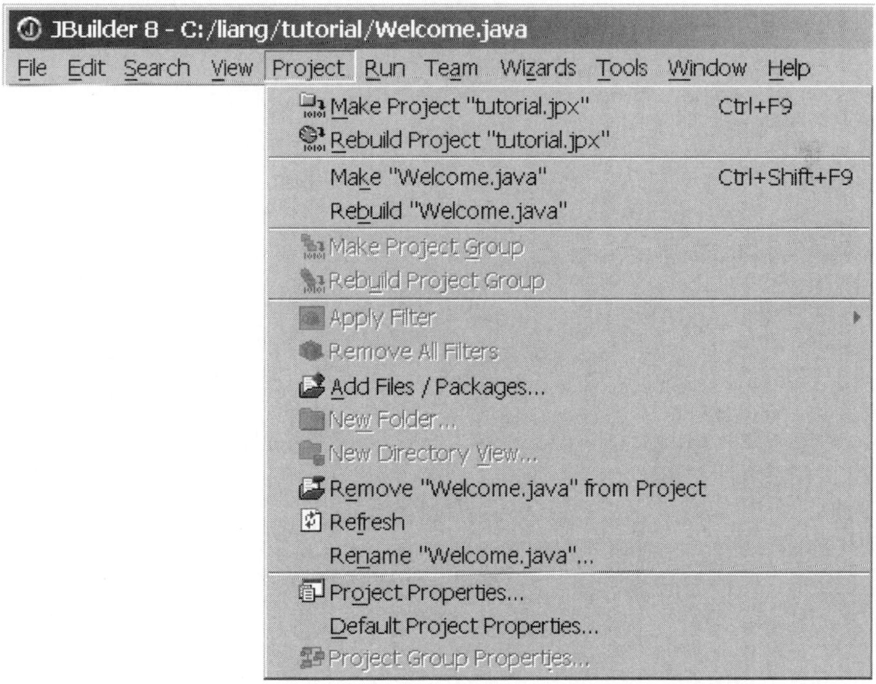

Figure 7.10   *The Project menu contains the commands for processing and managing projects.*

7.6 The Run Commands

The Run menu (see Figure 7.11) contains the commands used for running and debugging your applications or applets from the IDE. The Debugging commands will be introduced in Chapter 8, "Debugging in JBuilder."

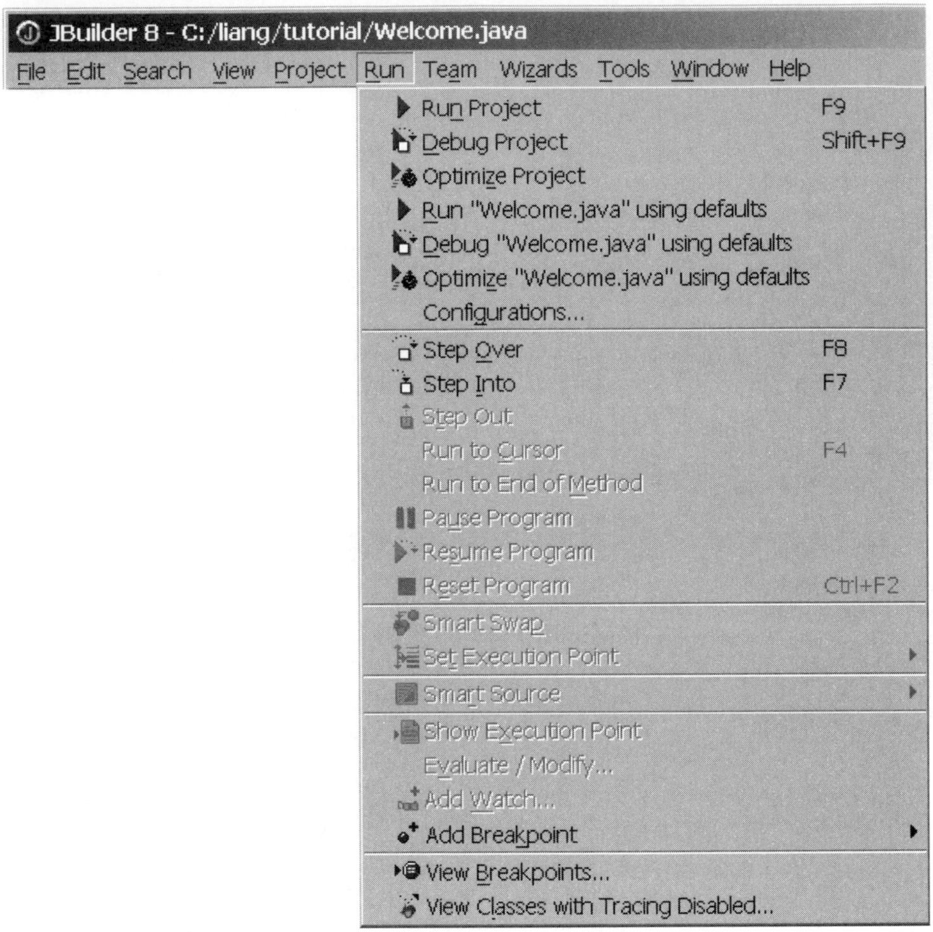

Figure 7.11 *The Run menu contains the commands for running and debugging programs.*

CHAPTER 8

Debugging in JBuilder

Debugging is finding errors (i.e., *bugs*) in a program and correcting them. Programming errors can be separated into syntax errors, runtime errors, and logic errors. Runtime errors that cause a program to abort are reported by the Java runtime system. Syntax errors are detected and reported by the compiler. In general, errors of these two kinds are easy to locate and fix. Therefore, debugging usually means to find logic errors.

Logic errors result in incorrect output or cause a program to terminate unexpectedly. To find logic errors, you can *hand trace* the program (i.e., catch errors by reading the program) or insert print statements in order to show the values of the variables or the execution flow of the program. This approach might work for a short, simple program. But for a large, complex program, the most effective approach for debugging is to use a debugger utility. This chapter introduces debugging in JBuilder.

8.1 General Debugging Techniques

Debugger utilities let you trace the execution of a program. They differ from one system to another, but all of them support most of the following helpful features:

- **Executing a single statement at a time**: The debugger allows you to execute one statement at a time so that you can see the effect of each statement.
- **Tracing into or stepping over a method**: If a method is being executed, you can ask the debugger to enter it and execute one statement at a time, or you can ask it to step over the entire method. You should step over the entire method if you know the method works. For example, always step over system-supplied methods like `System.out.println()`.
- **Setting breakpoints**: You can also set a breakpoint at a specific statement. When your program reaches a breakpoint, it pauses and displays the line with the breakpoint. You can set as many breakpoints as you want. Breakpoints are especially useful when you know where your programming error begins. You can set a breakpoint at that line and have the program execute until it reaches the breakpoint.

- **Displaying variables**: The debugger lets you select several variables and display their values. As you trace through a program, the contents of the variables are continuously updated.
- **Using call stacks**: The debugger lets you trace all of the method calls and lists all pending methods. This feature is helpful when you need to see a large picture of the program execution flow.
- **Modifying variables**: Some debuggers enable you to modify the value of a variable when debugging. This is convenient when you want to test a program with different samples but do not want to leave the debugger.

The debugger utility is integrated in JBuilder. You can pinpoint bugs in your program with the help of the JBuilder debugger without leaving the IDE. The JBuilder debugger enables you to set breakpoints and execute programs line by line. As your program executes, you can watch the values stored in variables, observe which methods are being called, and know what events have occurred in the program.

8.2 Starting the Debugger

To demonstrate debugging, this chapter uses the following class example. The class named **SelectionSort** contains the **selectionSort** method. Suppose a mistake is made in the **selectionSort** method, as shown in the following code listing at the highlighted line:

```
// SelectionSort.java: Sort numbers using selection sort
package tutorial;

public class SelectionSort {
  /** Main method */
  public static void main(String[] args) {
    // Initialize the list
    double[] myList = {5.0, 4.4, 1.9, 2.9, 3.4, 3.5};

    // Print the original list
    System.out.println("My list before sort is: ");
    printList(myList);

    // Sort the list
    selectionSort(myList);

    // Print the sorted list
    System.out.println();
    System.out.println("My list after sort is: ");
    printList(myList);
  }

  /** The method for printing numbers */
  static void printList(double[] list) {
    for (int i = 0; i < list.length; i++)
      System.out.print(list[i] + "  ");
    System.out.println();
  }
```

```
/** The method for sorting the numbers */
static void selectionSort(double[] list) {
  double currentMax;
  int currentMaxIndex;

  for (int i = list.length - 1; i >= 1; i--) {
    // Find the maximum in the list[0..i]
    currentMax = list[i];
    currentMaxIndex = i;

    for (int j = i - 1; j >= 0; j--) {
      if (currentMax < list[j]) {
        currentMax = list[i]; // list[i] should be list[j]
        currentMaxIndex = j;
      }
    }

    // Swap list[i] with list[currentMaxIndex] if necessary;
    if (currentMaxIndex != i) {
      list[currentMaxIndex] = list[i];
      list[i] = currentMax;
    }
  }
}
```

Note that **currentMax = list[i]** should be **currentMax = list[j]**. The programmer, however, is not aware of the mistake. The debugger helps to locate the error.

Perform the following steps to start debugging SelectionSort:

1. Click the cutter (gray column on the left edge of the content pane) of the first non-comment line in the *main* method to set a breakpoint, as shown in Figure 8.1. A solid circle is displayed at the cutter of the line.

2. Choose *SelectionSort.java* in the project pane and right-click the mouse button to display the context menu. Click *Debug using defaults* in the context menu to start debugging.

> *Note*: There are several ways to start the debugger. Steps 1 and 2 are the most convenient.

If the program compiles without problems, the message pane becomes a debugger window, as shown in Figure 8.2.

There are six tabs on the left side of the message pane: console view (■), stack view (▣), watch view (▣), loaded class view (▣), breakpoint view (▣), and class tracing view (▣). The *console view* displays output and errors and enables the user to enter input from the console. The *stack view* displays threads running in the program. The *watch view* displays the contents of the variables in the watch view. The loaded class view displays classes currently loaded by the program. The *class tracing view* displays classes with tracing disabled. This feature is not available in JBuilder Personal. It is only available in the Standard and Enterprise Edition of JBuilder. By default, tracing for the

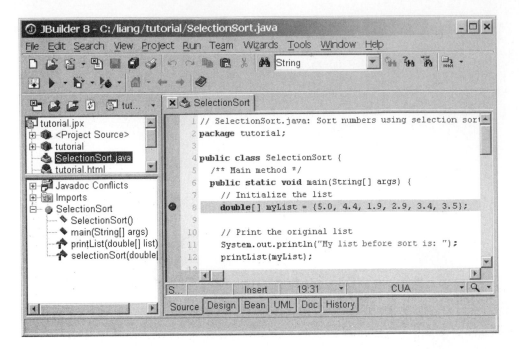

Figure 8.1   *A breakpoint is set at the first line of the main method.*

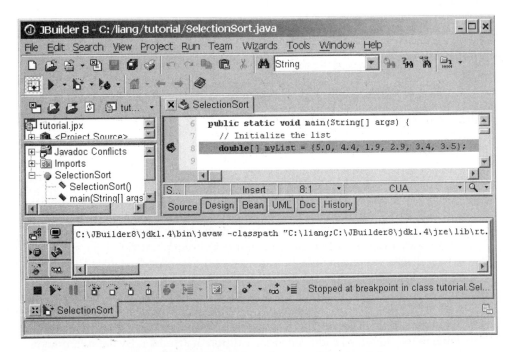

Figure 8.2   *The message pane became a debugger window.*

classes in the Java library is disabled. To enable tracing a Java library class, choose the package that contains the class, right-click the mouse to display a context menu. Click Remove to remove the package from the Class Tracing view.

8.3   Controlling Program Execution

The program pauses at the first line in the **main** method. This line, called the *current execution point*, is highlighted and has a green arrow to the left. The execution point marks the next line of source code to be executed by the debugger.

When the program pauses at the execution point, you can issue debugging commands to control the execution of the program. You also can inspect or modify the values of variables in the program.

When JBuilder is in the debugging mode, the Run menu contains the debugging commands (see Figure 8.3). Some of the commands also appear in the message pane. The message pane contains additional commands that are not in the Run menu. Here are the commands for controlling program execution:

- **Step Over** executes a single statement. If the statement contains a call to a method, the entire method is executed without stepping through it.

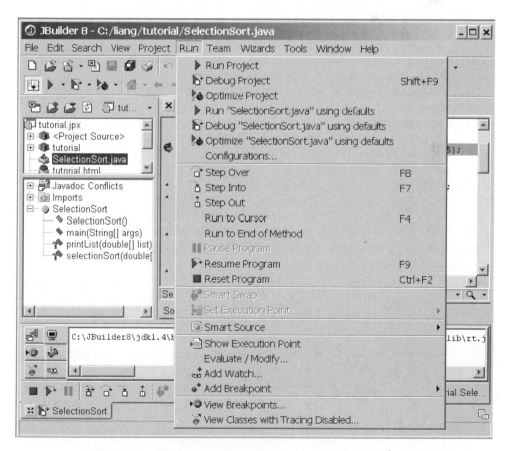

Figure 8.3   *The debugging commands appear under the Run menu.*

- **Step Into** executes a single statement or steps into a method.
- **Step Out** executes all the statements in the current method and returns to its caller.
- **Run to Cursor** runs the program, starting from the current execution point, and pauses and places the execution point on the line of code containing the cursor, or at a breakpoint.
- **Run to End of Method** runs the program until it reaches the end of the current method or a breakpoint.
- **Resume Program** continues the current debugging session or restarts one that has finished or been reset.
- **Reset Program** ends the current program and releases it from memory. Use Reset to restart an application from the beginning, as when you make a change to the code and want to run again from the beginning, or if variables or data structures become corrupted with unwanted values. This command terminates debugging and returns to the normal editing session.
- **Show Execution Point** positions the cursor at the execution point in the content pane.

8.4   Examining and Modifying Data Values

Among the most powerful features of an integrated debugger is its capability to reveal current data values and enable programmers to modify values during debugging. You can examine the values of variables, array items, and objects, or the values of the parameters passed in a method call. You also can modify a variable value if you want to try a new value to continue debugging without restarting the program.

JBuilder provides the commands Add Watch and Evaluate/Modify to enable you to inspect and modify the values of variables. These commands can be issued from the Run menu or by clicking the right mouse button on the variable in the Watch view or in the source code.

8.4.1   The Add Watch Command

The Add Watch command adds variables to the Watch view so that you can watch the changing values of variables while debugging. You can view the Watch view by selecting the Watch tab at the bottom of the structure pane. To add the variable `myList` in the `SelectionSort` to the Watch view, perform the following steps:

1. Suppose the execution point is currently at the first line in the main method. Highlight `myList` in the code and right-click the mouse to reveal a popup menu.
2. Choose *Add Watch* in the popup menu to bring up a dialog box, as shown in Figure 8.4. Click *OK* to add `myList` to the Watch list.
3. Choose the Watch tab at the left side of the message pane. The Watch view is shown in Figure 8.5.
4. Choose *Run*, *Step Over* to observe the changing value of `myList` in the Watch view.

Figure 8.4   *The Add Watch dialog box enables you to add a variable to the Watch view.*

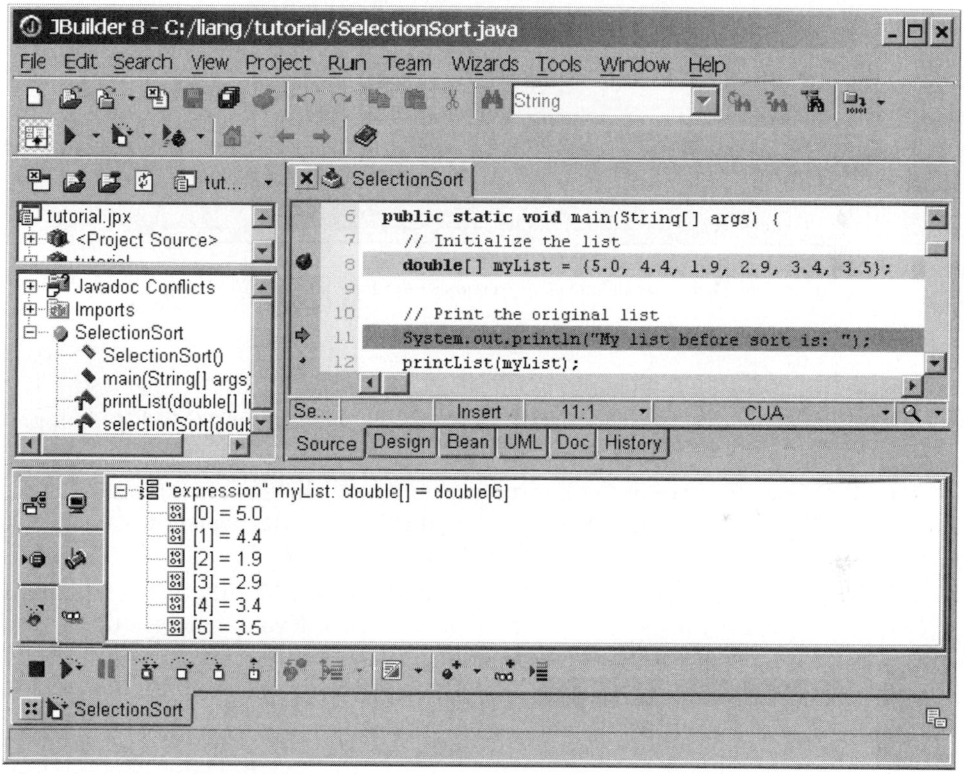

Figure 8.5   *The variable* `myList` *was added to the Watch view.*

8.4.2   The Evaluate/Modify Command

The Evaluate/Modify command opens an Evaluate/Modify window where you can enter an expression and evaluate it. This is helpful for gathering additional information about the variable values in the program. The following steps show you how to evaluate an expression:

1. Set the cursor anywhere inside the second **for** loop in the **selectionSort** method.
2. Choose *Run, Run to Cursor* to execute the program at full speed until it reaches the cursor.

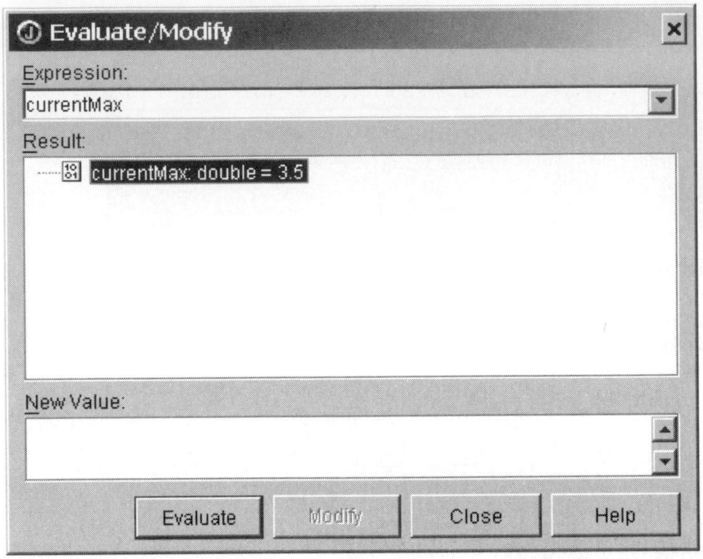

Figure 8.6   *You can evaluate an expression in the Evaluate/Modify dialog box.*

3. Choose *Run*, *Evaluate/Modify* to bring up the Evaluate/Modify dialog box, as shown in Figure 8.6.

4. Type `currentMax` in the Expression field, and click Evaluate to see the result in the Result field. You can modify currentMax by entering a new value in the New Value field and click Modify to activate the change.

5. You can also evaluate expression in the Evaluate/Modify dialog box. For example, type `i < j` in the Expression field, and click Evaluate to see the result in the Result field, as shown in Figure 8.7.

6. Click *Done* to close the window.

8.5   Setting Breakpoints

You can execute a program line by line to trace it, but this is time-consuming if you are debugging a large program. Often, you know that some parts of the program work fine. It makes no sense to trace these parts when you only need to trace the lines of code that are likely to have bugs. In cases of this kind, you can use breakpoints.

A *breakpoint* is a stop sign placed on a line of source code that tells the debugger to pause when this line is encountered. The debugger executes every line until it encounters a breakpoint, so you can trace the part of the program at the breakpoint. Using the breakpoint, you can quickly move over the sections you know work correctly and concentrate on the sections causing problems.

There are several ways to set a breakpoint on a line. One quick way is to click the cutter of the line on which you want to put a breakpoint. You will see the line

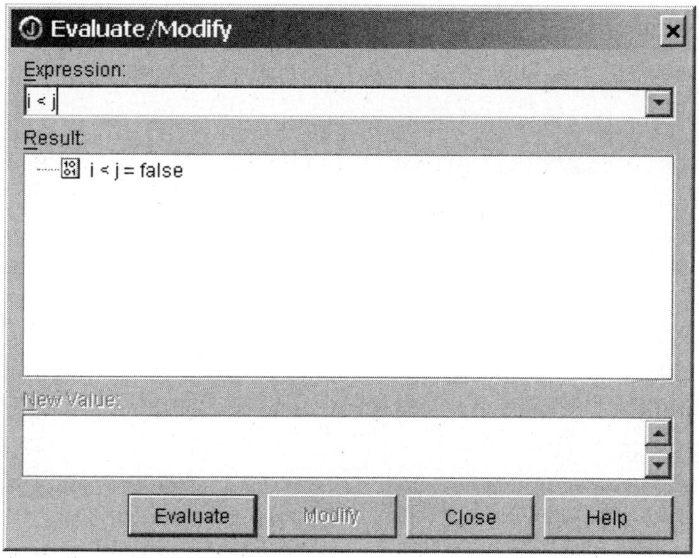

Figure 8.7   *You can evaluate an expression in the Evaluate/Modify dialog box.*

highlighted, as shown in Figure 8.1. You also can set breakpoints by choosing *Run, Add Breakpoint*. To remove a breakpoint, simply click the cutter of the line.

As you debug your program, you can set as many breakpoints as you want, and can remove breakpoints at any time during debugging. The project retains the breakpoints you have set when you exit the project. The breakpoints are restored when you reopen it.

8.6   Debugging SelectionSort

Use the debugger to uncover the bugs in SelectionSort by performing the following steps:

1. Since you know there is nothing wrong in the code before invoking the **selectionSort** method, you can skip the lines before calling **selectionSort** in the **main** method by setting a breakpoint at the line for **selectionSort(myList)**, as shown in Figure 8.8.

2. Choose SelectionSort.java in the project pane. Right click it to display the context menu. Choose *Debug using defaults* to debug the program. The debugger executes all lines until it reaches to the breakpoint.

3. Choose *Run, Step Into* to debug the **selectionSort** method.

4. Add **list** and **currentMax** to the watch view and select the watch tab to monitor **list**. Check whether **list** has the correct initial values before the method starts (see Figure 8.9).

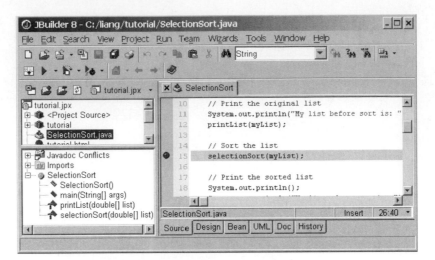

Figure 8.8 *Set a breakpoint at where the problem is.*

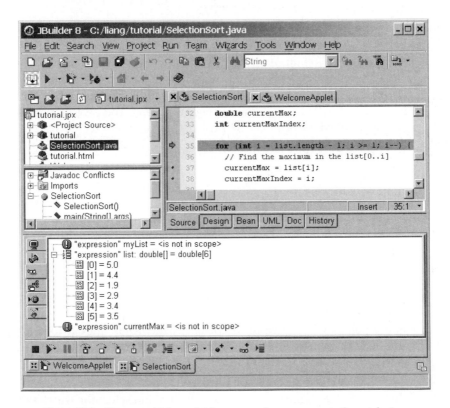

Figure 8.9 *You can add the variables* `list` *and* `currentMax` *to the watch view.*

5. The `selectionSort()` method places the largest number at the end of the list after an iteration of the outer `for` loop. Run through the iteration at full speed by setting the cursor at the `if` statement for swapping numbers, then choose *Run*, *Run to Cursor*.

6. Examine the value of `currentMax` in the Watch view, as shown in Figure 8.10. Clearly, `currentMax` is not getting the correct value. The correct value should be 5.0. Assign `list[j]` to `currentMax`, not `list[i]`.

7. Change `list[i]` to `list[j]` and choose *Run*, *Step Over*. A dialog box prompts you to recompile and restart debugging. Click *Yes* to continue. JBuilder recompiles and restarts the debugger.

Tip: The debugger is an indispensable, powerful tool that boosts your programming productivity. It may take you some time to become familiar with it, but your investment will pay off in the long run.

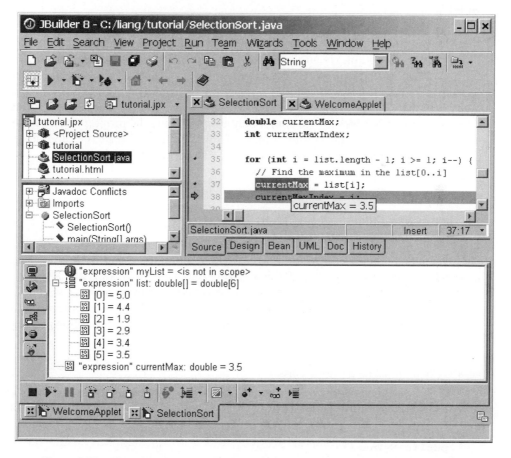

Figure 8.10 *The value of* `currentMax` *reveals incorrect max in the* `selectionSort` *method.*

C H A P T E R   9

Designing User Interfaces Using JBuilder UI Designer

JBuilder provides the UI Designer for visually designing and programming Java classes. This enables you to quickly and easily assemble the elements of a user interface (UI) for a Java application or applet. You can construct the UI with various building blocks chosen from the component palette, which contains such components as buttons, text areas, lists, dialogs, and menus. Then you set the values of the component properties and attach event-handler code to the component events, telling the program how to respond to UI events. JBuilder's UI Designer makes programming in Java easier and more productive. This chapter demonstrates the use of visual design tools to rapidly develop GUI programs.

9.1   JavaBeans and JBuilder UI Designer

JavaBeans is a software component architecture that extends the power of the Java language by enabling well-formed objects to be manipulated visually at design time in a pure Java builder tool, such as JBuilder, WebGain Café, or IBM Visual Age for Java. Such well-formed objects are referred to as *JavaBeans* or simply *beans*. The classes that define the beans, referred to as *JavaBeans components* or *bean components*, or simply *components*, conform to the JavaBeans component model with the following requirements:

- A bean must be a public class.
- A bean must have a public default constructor (one that takes no arguments), though it can have other constructors, if needed. For example, a bean named **MyBean** must either have a constructor with the signature

  ```
  public MyBean();
  ```

  or have no constructor if its superclass has a default constructor.

- A bean must implement the **java.io.Serializable** or **java.io.Externalizable** interface to ensure a persistent state. JavaBeans can be used in a wide variety of tools, such as Lotus, Delphi, MS Visual Basic, and MS Word. When JavaBeans are used in other tools, bean persistence may be required. Some tools need to save the beans and restore them later. Bean persistence ensures that the tools can reconstruct the properties and consistent behaviors of the bean to the state at which it was saved.
- A bean usually has properties with correctly constructed public accessor methods that enable the properties to be seen and updated visually by a builder tool.
- A bean may have events with correctly constructed public registration methods that enable the bean to add and remove listeners. If the bean plays a role as the source of events, it must provide registration methods for registering listeners. For example, you can register a listener for **ActionEvent** using the **addActionListener** method of a **JButton** bean.

The first three requirements must be observed by the beans, and therefore are referred to as *minimum JavaBeans component requirements*. The last two requirements are dependent on implementations. It is possible to write a bean without accessor methods and event-registration methods.

A JavaBean component is a special kind of Java class. The relationship between JavaBean components and Java classes is illustrated in Figure 9.1.

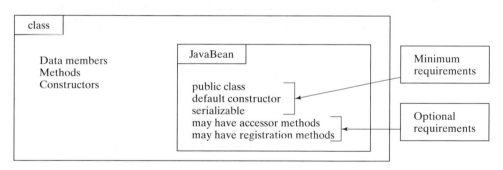

Figure 9.1 *A JavaBean component is a serializable public class with a default constructor.*

The getter method is named **get<PropertyName>()**, which takes no parameters and returns an object of a type identical to the property type. For example, **getContentPane()** is the getter method for the property **contentPane** in the **JFrame** class, which returns an object of the **Container** type. For a property of the **boolean** type, the getter method should be named **is<PropertyName>()**, which returns a **boolean** value. For example, **isVisible()** is the getter method for the **visible** property in the **JFrame** class, which returns **true** if the frame is visible.

The setter method is named **set<PropertyName>**, which takes a single parameter identical to the property type and returns **void**. For example, **setLayout** is the setter method for the **layout** property in the **Container** class for setting the **layout** property value.

You can retrieve these properties using the getter methods and modify them using the setter methods. The principal benefit of JavaBeans is for use in the Java builder tools for rapid Java application development. As shown in Figure 9.2, you can set the properties of a **JButton** instance in JBuilder's visual designer during design time.

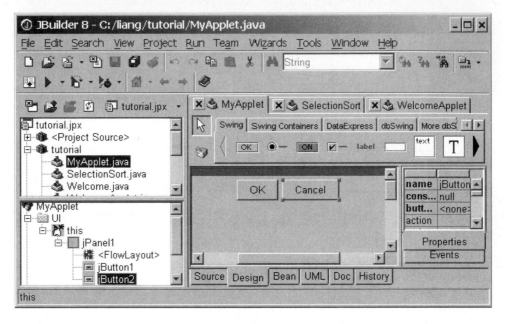

Figure 9.2   *You can set the properties of a JavaBeans instance, such as a* **JButton,** *at design time.*

JBuilder provides tools for visually designing and programming Java classes. This enables you to quickly and easily assemble the elements of a user interface (UI) for a Java application or applet. You can construct the UI with various building blocks chosen from the component palette. To display the component palette, select a .java file in the navigation pane, and choose the Design tab in the content pane. The component palette, as shown in Figure 9.2, contains visual components for rapid application development. The components are grouped into eleven groups with the tab names Swing, Swing Containers, DataExpress, dbSwing, More dbSwing, db-Swing Models, InternetBeans, XML, EJB, AWT, CORBA, XML, EJB and Other in the Enterprise Edition of JBuilder. If you are using JBuilder 7 Personal, the component palette may not contain all these components. You click a tab to select a group of components. JBuilder has an intelligent click-and-drop capability that enables you to click a button or some other component from the Swing group, then drop it into the user interface. You then set the values of the component properties and attach event-handler code to the component events, telling the program how to respond to UI events.

JBuilder's visual tools make programming in Java easier and more productive. Since tools cannot do everything, however, you will have to modify the programs they produce. This makes it imperative to know the basic concepts of Java GUI programming before starting to use visual tools.

JBuilder's visual tools are designed to work well with class templates created with JBuilder wizards. Use the Application wizard, the Applet wizard, and the other wizards in the object gallery to create classes to work with the JBuilder visual design tools. Since JBuilder synchronizes visual designing with the source code, any changes you make in the designer are automatically reflected in the source code. Likewise, any changes to the source code that affect the visual interface are also reflected in the visual designer. This synchronization enables you to build Java programs by editing the source code or using the visual designer, whichever is more convenient.

9.2 Developing Programs Using UI Designer

When using visual designers to develop a project, carefully plan the project before implementing it. The major part of the planning involves the design of the user interface. Draw a sketch of the layout that shows all the visible components you plan to use.

Implementation is a two-step process that involves creating a user interface and writing code. To create a user interface, click-and-drop the components, such as a **JButton** or a **JLabel**, from the component palette to the frame or applet and set the component's properties through the component inspector. Write code to implement event handlers to carry out the actions required by the applications.

This section demonstrates the use of visual design tools in JBuilder in developing a program that performs addition, subtraction, multiplication, and division using the Add, Subtract, Multiply, and Divide buttons and the menu commands Add, Subtract, Multiply, and Divide from the Operation menu, as shown in Figure 9.3.

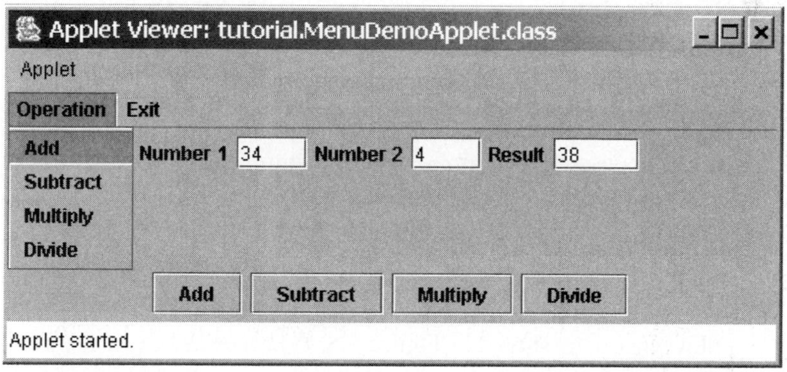

Figure 9.3 *The program lets the user enter numbers and perform addition, subtraction, multiplication, and division.*

The task for completing this application is divided into three phases:

1. Create a user interface, as shown in Figure 9.4.

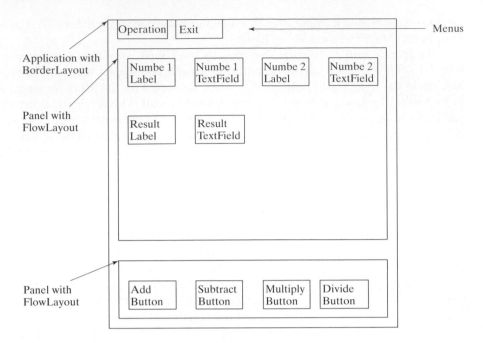

Figure 9.4 *The panel containing the labels and text fields is placed in the center of the application, and the panel containing the buttons is placed in the south of the application.*

2. Implement handlers to carry out the actions of the Add, Subtract, Multiply, and Divide buttons.
3. Create and implement the menu commands for Add, Subtract, Multiply, and Divide in the Operation menu, and for Close in the Exit menu.

Phase 1: Creating User Interface

The user interface in Figure 9.4 consists of labels and text boxes in a panel with **FlowLayout** and four buttons in another panel with **FlowLayout**. The two panels are placed in the applet using **BorderLayout** (see Figure 9.3.) The following are the steps in creating the user interface for Figure 9.3.

1. Create an applet as follows:
   1.1. In the tutorial.jpx project, choose *File*, *New* to display the object gallery. Click the Applet icon in the Web page of the object gallery to display the Applet wizard, as shown in Figure 9.5. Type **tutorial** in the Package field and **MenuDemoApplet** in the Class field, choose javax.swing.JApplet in the Base class field, and check "Can run standalone." Click *Finish* to generate templates of an .html file and a .java file.
2. Start the UI designer as follows. With MenuDemoApplet.java selected in the project pane, choose the Design tab in the content pane. You will see the UI designer appear in the content pane, as shown in Figure 9.6. The component tree appears in the structure pane to display a structured view of all the components in your source file (and their relationships). You can use it to navigate through

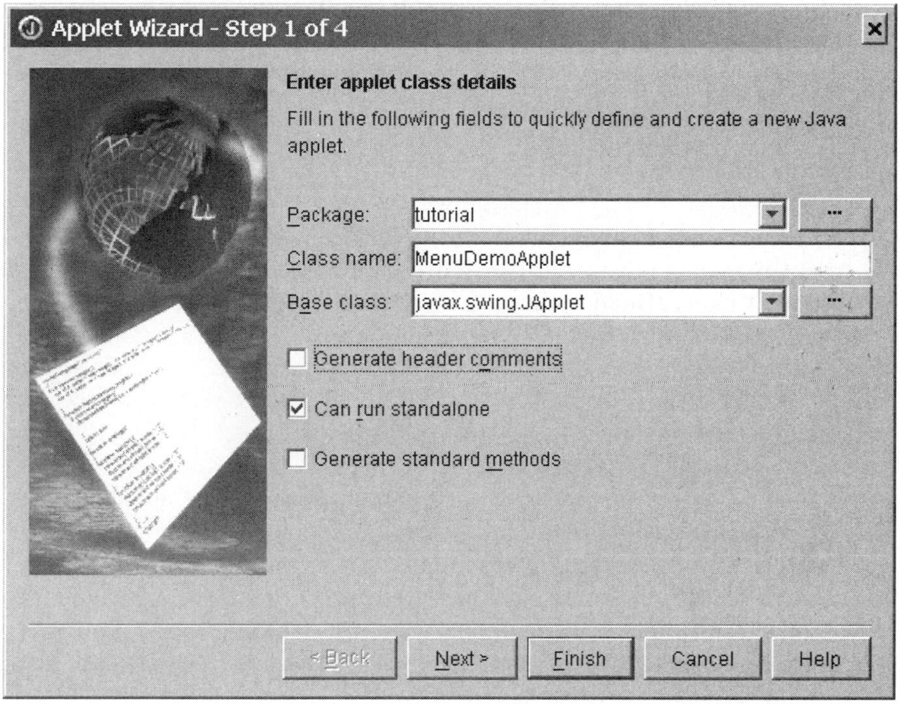

Figure 9.5   *The Applet wizard creates an HTML file and a Java applet template.*

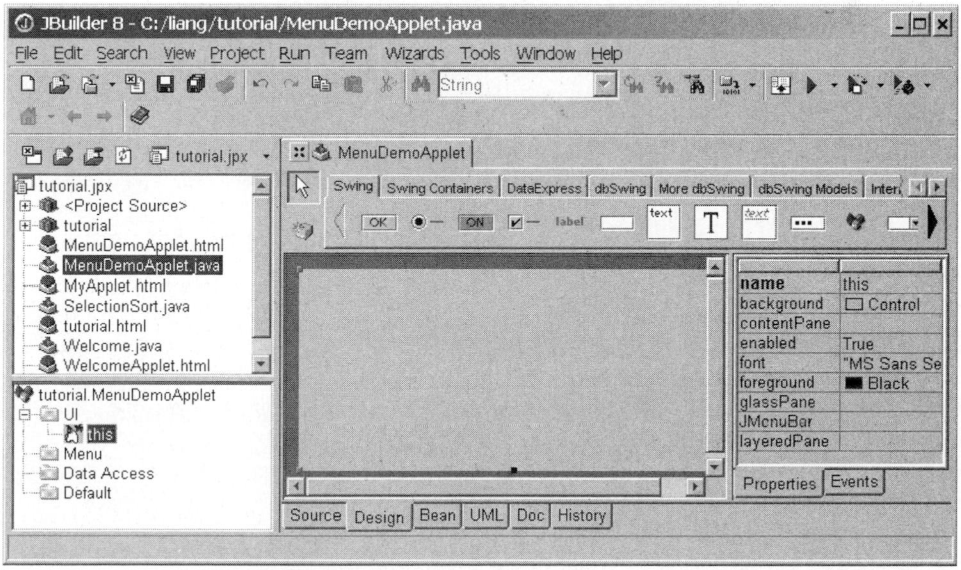

Figure 9.6   *The UI Designer is displayed in the content pane.*

the components in the UI designer. You will also see the component inspector pane displayed inside the content pane. The component inspector is used to inspect and set the values of component properties and to attach methods to component events. Changes made in the component inspector are reflected visually in the UI designer. When you highlight a component in the component tree, the component is highlighted in the UI designer, and is displayed in the component inspector.

3. On the Swing Containers tab of the component palette, click the **JPanel** icon (the first icon in this group), then drop it into the center of the UI designer in the content pane. JBuilder creates an instance of **JPanel** named **jPanel1**. You can see **jPanel1** in the component tree under the node **this**, as shown in Figure 9.7. **jPanel1** will be used to hold the labels and text fields. You can also see the code for creating **jPanel1** in the program source code. To see the source code, choose the Source tab in the content pane, as shown in Figure 9.8.

> *Note*: **jPanel1** was added into the content pane of the applet. By default, the content pane uses **BorderLayout**.

4. You need to create a second panel in the applet to hold the action buttons: Add, Subtract, Multiply, and Divide. Here are the steps in creating this panel.
   4.1. Switch back to the UI designer by clicking the Design tab and select the node **this** in the component tree.
   4.2. Click the **JPanel** icon on the Swing Containers page of the component palette and drop it to the node **this** on the component tree to create

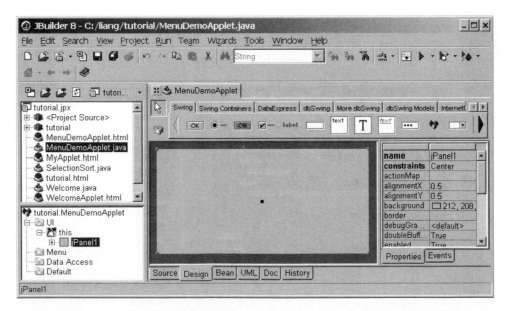

Figure 9.7   *The* **javax.swing.JPanel** *was added to the UI designer to create* **jPanel1**.

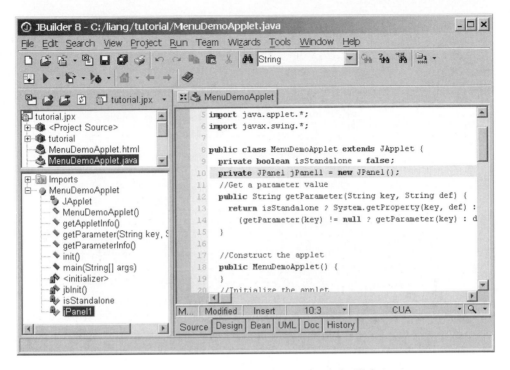

Figure 9.8 *The source code is synchronized with the UI designer.*

jPanel2. You will see **jPanel2** appearing under the node **this** in the component tree, as shown in Figure 9.9.

5. Set the properties for **jPanel1** and **jPanel2**.

   5.1. With **jPanel1** selected in the component tree, set its **constraints** to **Center** in the component inspector. By default, panels use **FlowLayout**. Since you will use **FlowLayout** for panels in this example, there is no need to set the **layout** property.

   5.2. With **jPanel2** selected in the component tree, set its **constraints** to **South** in the component inspector.

6. Create labels and text fields in **jPanel1**.

   6.1. To create the label Number 1 in **jPanel1**, click the **JLabel** icon on the Swing page of the component palette. Drop it into **jPanel1** in the UI designer. This action creates a label named **jLabel1** in **jPanel1**. In the component inspector for **jLabel1**, set the **text** property to Number 1 and change the **name** property to **jlblNum1**. You will see Number 1 in the UI designer and **jlblNum1** as the new name for **jLable1** in the component tree.

   6.2. To place a text field in **jPanel1**, click the **JTextField** icon in the Swing page, and drop it into **jPanel1** after the label Number 1. This action creates

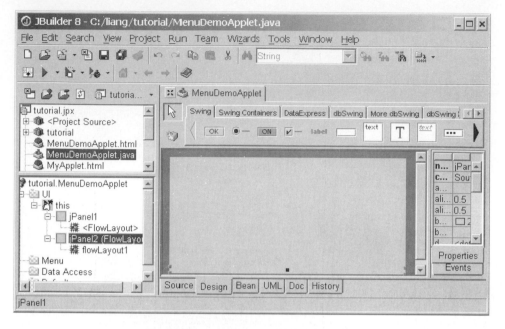

Figure 9.9   `jPanel2` *was added to the applet.*

a `JTextField` named `jTextField1` in `jPanel1`. In the component inspector for `jTextField1`, set the `column` property to 4, `text` property to empty, and change the `name` property to `jtfNum1`. You will see `jtfNum1` as the new name for `jTextField1` in the component tree.

6.3. Similarly, you can create a label Number 2, a text field for Number 2, a label Result, and a text field for Result in `jPanel1`, as shown in Figure 9.10. Name the labels `jlblNum2` and `jlblResult` and the text fields `jtfNum2` and `jtfResult`.

7. Create buttons in the panel `jPanel2`.

7.1. To create the Add button in `jPanel2`, select `jPanel2` in the component tree, click the `JButton` icon in the Swing page of the component palette and drop it into `jPanel2` in the UI designer. This action creates `jButton1` and adds it to `jPanel2`. In the component inspector for `jButton1`, set the `text` property to Add and change the `name` property to `jbtAdd`. You will see the button with the caption Add in the UI designer and `jbtAdd` as the new name for `jButton1` in the component tree.

> *Tip*: If you don't see the caption Add, click `jPanel2` in the component tree twice to refresh the UI designer. If the problem remains, close the file in the content pane, and then reopen the file in the navigation pane.

7.2. Other buttons, such as Subtract, Multiply, and Divide, can also be created (see Figure 9.11).

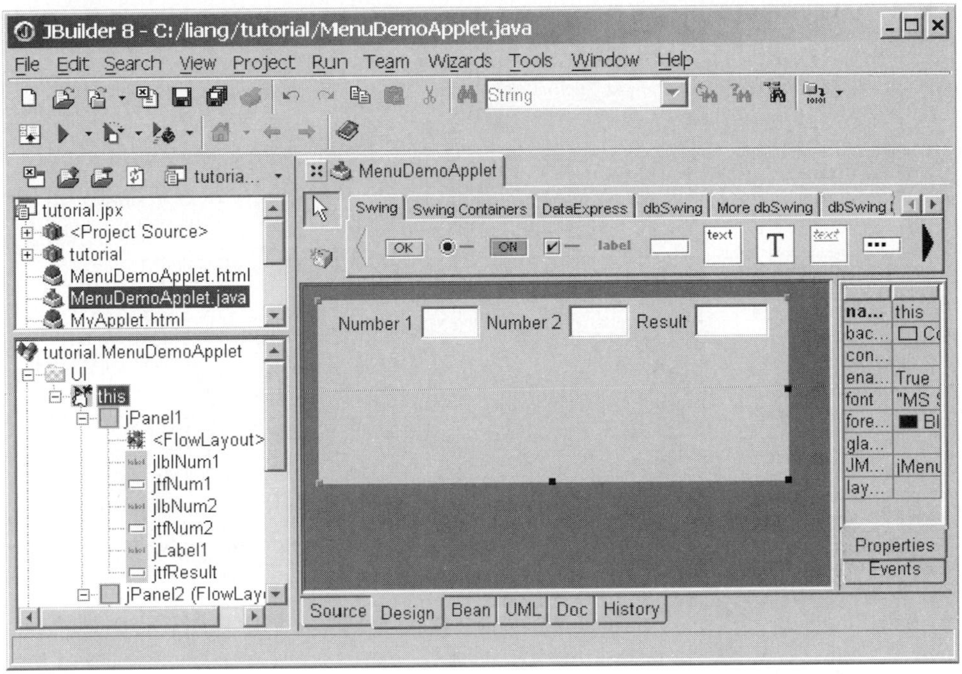

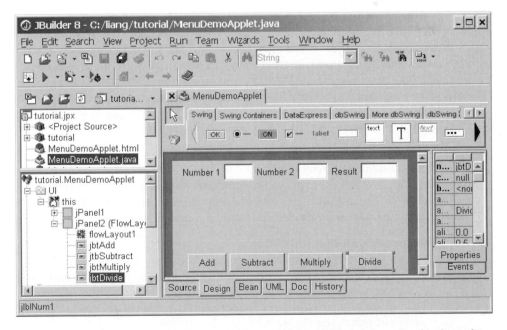

Figure 9.10   *The labels and text fields were added to* `jPanel1`*.*

Figure 9.11   *The UI components were placed in the panels, and the panels were placed in the applet.*

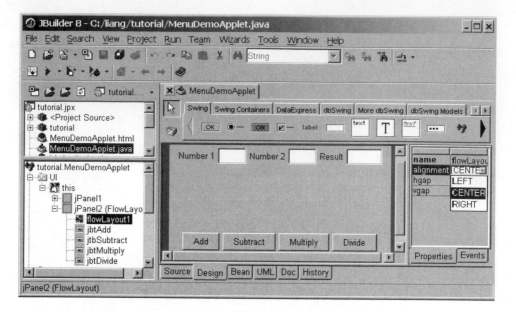

Figure 9.12 *You can use the component inspector to change the attributes of a layout manager.*

Tip: For safety, you should save your work frequently by choosing *File*, *Save All* to save all the files before proceeding.

Tip: JBuilder also allows you to change the attributes of the layout manager from the component inspector. If you want to change the attributes in the **FlowLayout** manager in **jPanel2**, change the **layout** property of **jPanel2** to **FlowLayout** to create an instance of the **FlowLayout** named **flowLayout1**, as shown in Figure 9.12. Select **flowLayout1** under the node **jPanel2** in the component tree. You can specify the alignment using the **alignment** property, and set the vertical and horizontal gaps using the **vgap** and **hgap** properties in the component inspector.

Phase 2: Implementing Event Handlers

If you run this program now, you will see the user interface on the applet; but you cannot perform any calculations because no code is associated with the action buttons. You can add the code for handling the button actions as follows:

1. Add a handler for the Add button.

 1.1. Click the Design tab to switch to the UI designer (if necessary). Double-click the Add button. JBuilder automatically creates a handler method named **jbtAdd_actionPerformed** in the program. You can see that JBuilder points to the **jbtAdd_actionPerformed** method in the program source code of the content pane (see Figure 9.13).

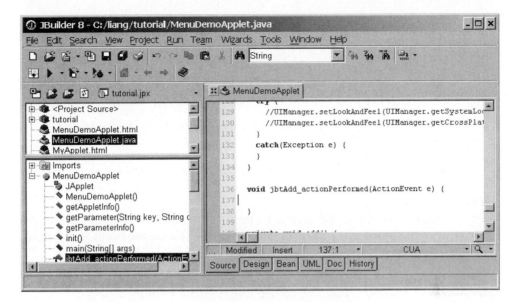

Figure 9.13   *JBuilder creates a method for handling button action.*

> *Note*: You know that the handler for button action is `actionPerformed`.
> Why does JBuilder create `jbtAdd_actionPerformed`? If you browse
> to the source code in the `jbInit` method, you will see that JBuilder
> added an anonymous adapter to handle the Add button action event,
> as follows:

```
jbtAdd.addActionListener(new
  java.awt.event.ActionListener() {
   public void actionPerformed(ActionEvent e) {
     jbtAdd_actionPerformed(e);
   }
});
```

You can choose anonymous adapter or standard adapter in the
Generated tab of the *Formatting* page of the Project Properties dialog
box, as shown in Figure 9.14.

1.2. Add the following code into the `jbtAdd_actionPerformed` method.

```
add();
```

1.3. Insert a new method `add()` after the `jbtAdd_actionPerformed` method in
the source code, as follows:

```
private void add() {
   // Use trim() to trim extraneous space in the text field
```

```
int num1 = Integer.parseInt(jtfNum1.getText().trim());
int num2 = Integer.parseInt(jtfNum2.getText().trim());
int result = num1 + num2;

// Set result in JTextField jtfResult
jtfResult.setText(String.valueOf(result));
}
```

2. Run the program to see how it works so far. Fix errors if necessary.

The handlers for other buttons can be added the same way. Omit these handlers for the time being and proceed to the next section to learn how to use the Menu designer.

Phase 3: Creating Menus

In this section, you will add menus to perform the same operations as the buttons. Menus can be added using the Menu designer, an easy-to-use tool for designing comprehensive menu interfaces.

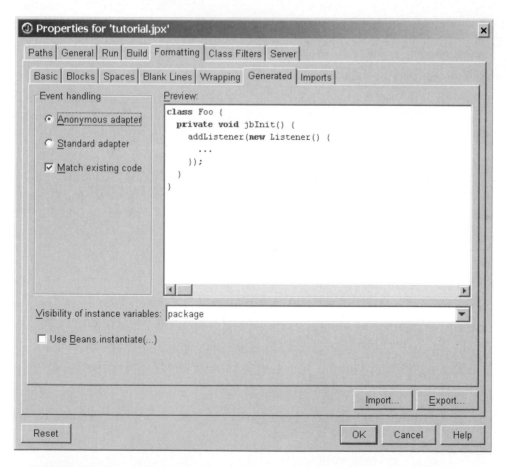

Figure 9.14   *You can choose anonymous adapter or standard adapter for generating handlers.*

The following are the steps in creating menus and implementing menu handlers:

1. Switch to the UI designer and drop a **JMenuBar** from the Swing Containers page of the component palette to the UI designer. You will see **jMenuBar1** appearing under the Menu node in the component tree, as shown in Figure 9.15.

2. Double-click **jMenuBar1** to start the Menu designer, as shown in Figure 9.16.

3. Add an Operation menu and its menu items.

   3.1. Highlight the first menu, type **Operation**, then press the Enter key.

   3.2. The first menu item under Operation is automatically highlighted. Type **Add** and press Enter.

   3.3. The next menu item after Add is highlighted automatically. Type **Subtract** and press Enter.

   3.4. The next menu item after Subtract is highlighted automatically. Type **Multiply** and press Enter.

   3.5. The next menu item after Multiply is highlighted automatically. Type **Divide** and press Enter.

   3.6. Highlight the menu to the right of Operation. Type **Exit** and press Return.

   3.7. Highlight the menu item under Exit. Type **Close** and press Enter.

   The menus are added to the Menu designer, as shown in Figure 9.17. The changes are reflected automatically in the component tree and the source code.

4. Rename the menus. JBuilder creates variables for the menus and menu items you just typed. The variables are **jMenu1** for the Operation menu and **jMenuItem1** for the Add menu. You can change these to more descriptive names.

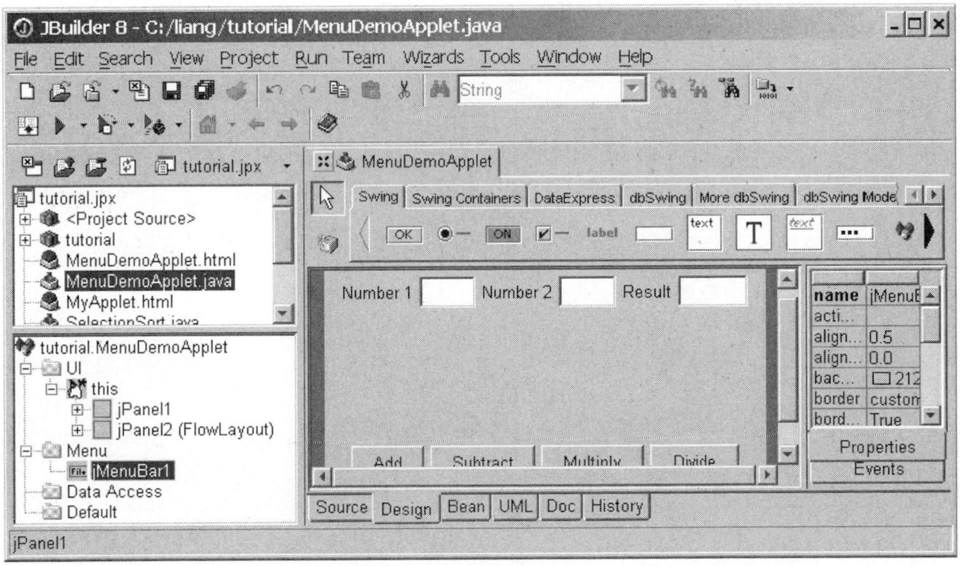

Figure 9.15   *An instance of* **JMenuBar** *was created in the applet.*

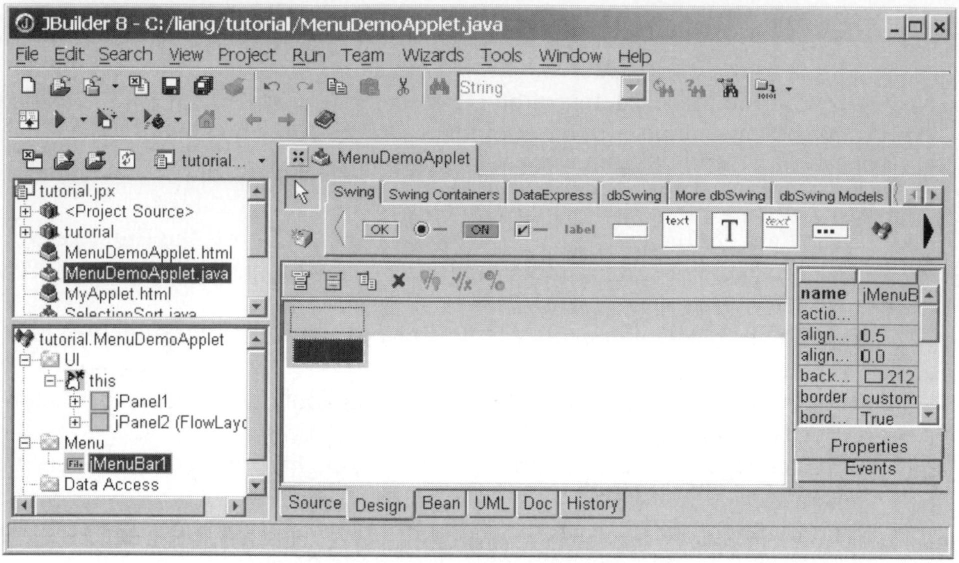

Figure 9.16   *The Menu designer is shown in the content pane.*

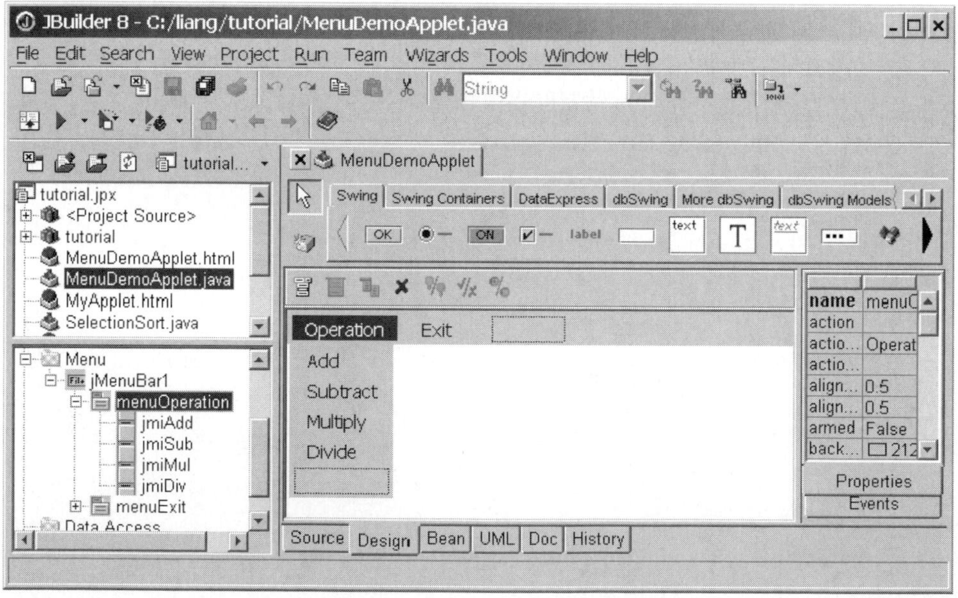

Figure 9.17   *The Operation and Exit menus (and their menu items) were created in the Menu designer.*

4.1. Click the Operation menu in either the component tree or the Menu designer to reveal its properties in the component inspector. Change the **name** property to **menuOperation**.

4.2. Similarly, set the menu item names to **jmiAdd**, **jmiSub**, **jmiMul**, and **jmiDiv** for the menu items Add, Subtract, Multiply, and Divide.

4.3. Set the names for Exit and Close to **menuExit** and **jmiClose**.

5. Implement menu handlers.

5.1. Highlight the menu item **jmiAdd** in the component tree to reveal its properties in the component inspector.

5.2. Choose the Events tab at the bottom of the component inspector (see Figure 9.18).

5.3. Point the mouse at the **actionPerformed** value field on the right, then press Enter. JBuilder automatically generates a method for handling the Add menu item. You can immediately see the method in the source code, as shown in Figure 9.19.

5.4. Simply add the following statement in the method body:

```
add();
```

Because **add()** has already been implemented in the source code, the program is ready to run. Run the program to see how the menus are working. You will not see the menu yet. The following step sets **jMenuBar1** as the menu bar for the applet.

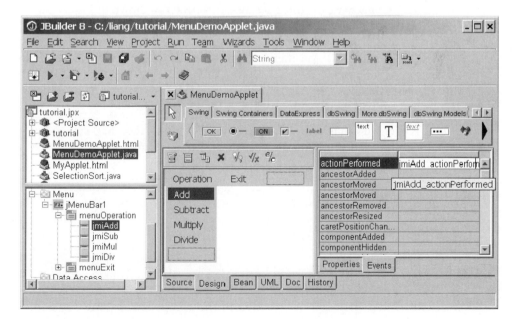

Figure 9.18 *Click the Event tab in the component inspector to display the event handlers associated with the component.*

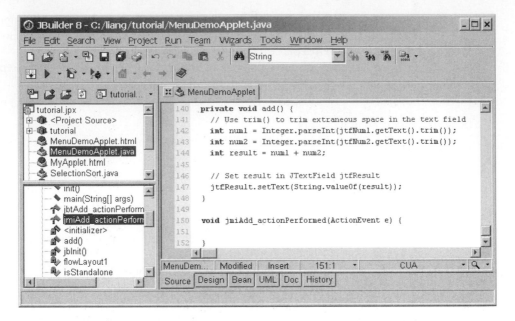

Figure 9.19 *JBuilder creates a method for handling menu item click actions.*

6. Click **this** under the UI node in the component tree to switch to the UI design-er. Select **jMenuBar1** for the **JMenuBar** property, as shown in Figure 9.20. If you run the program now, you will see the menus.

Note: If you don't see the menu at runtime, check whether the **this.set JMenuBar(jMenuBar1)** was created in the **jbInit** method. If not, close the file in the content pane, reopen it, and repeat Step 6.

Note: You can do many other things using the Menu designer, such as enter separator bars and shortcuts, disable (dim) a menu item or make it checkable, and create submenus.

Note: You can also view the applet within JBuilder. To do this, select MenuDe-moApplet.html in the navigation pane, and click the View tab in the content pane, as shown in Figure 9.21.

9.3 Installing and Using Custom Components

A JavaBeans component can be installed in the component palette. By default, fre-quently used Swing user interface components are preinstalled in the Swing tab and Swing Containers tab. This section demonstrates how to install a custom component and use it in the UI designer.

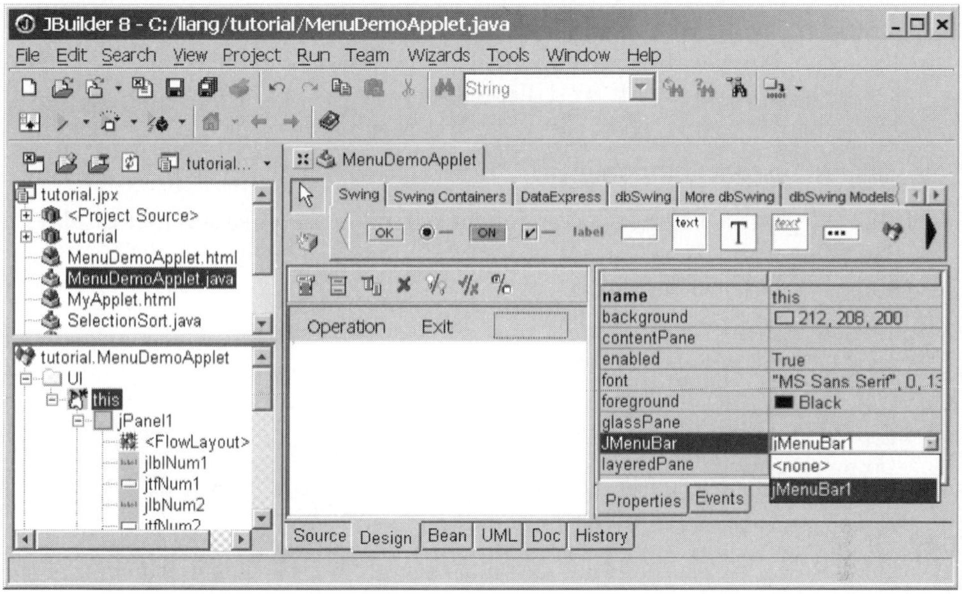

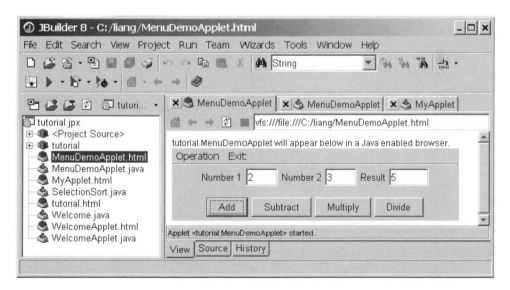

Figure 9.20   *The applet's* **JMenuBar** *property must be set for the menu to appear in the applet.*

Figure 9.21   *The applet can be viewed within JBuilder.*

> *Note*: A JavaBeans component is a public serializable class with a default constructor. Any JavaBeans component can be installed in the component palette regardless of whether it is GUI component or a non-GUI component.

9.3.1 Installing Custom Components

Listing 9.1 gives a JavaBeans component named **MessagePanel** that displays a message on a panel.

Listing 9.1: MessagePanel.java

```java
// MessagePanel.java: Display a message on a JPanel
package tutorial;

import java.awt.Font;
import java.awt.FontMetrics;
import java.awt.Dimension;
import java.awt.Graphics;
import javax.swing.JPanel;

public class MessagePanel extends JPanel {
  /** The message to be displayed */
  private String message = "Welcome to Java";

  /** The x coordinate where the message is displayed */
  private int xCoordinate = 20;

  /** The y coordinate where the message is displayed */
  private int yCoordinate = 20;

  /** Indicate whether the message is displayed in the center */
  private boolean centered;

  /** The interval for moving the message horizontally and
      vertically */
  private int interval = 10;

  /** Default constructor */
  public MessagePanel() {
  }

  /** Constructor with a message parameter */
  public MessagePanel(String message) {
    this.message = message;
  }

  /** Return message */
  public String getMessage() {
    return message;
  }

  /** Set a new message */
  public void setMessage(String message) {
    this.message = message;
    repaint();
  }
```

```java
/** Return xCoordinator */
public int getXCoordinate() {
  return xCoordinate;
}

/** Set a new xCoordinator */
public void setXCoordinate(int x) {
  this.xCoordinate = x;
  repaint();
}

/** Return yCoordinator */
public int getYCoordinate() {
  return yCoordinate;
}

/** Set a new yCoordinator */
public void setYCoordinate(int y) {
  this.yCoordinate = y;
  repaint();
}

/** Return centered */
public boolean isCentered() {
  return centered;
}

/** Set a new centered */
public void setCentered(boolean centered) {
  this.centered = centered;
  repaint();
}

/** Return interval */
public int getInterval() {
  return interval;
}

/** Set a new interval */
public void setInterval(int interval) {
  this.interval = interval;
  repaint();
}

/** Paint the message */
protected void paintComponent(Graphics g) {
  super.paintComponent(g);

  if (centered) {
    // Get font metrics for the current font
    FontMetrics fm = g.getFontMetrics();

    // Find the center location to display
    int stringWidth = fm.stringWidth(message);
    int stringAscent = fm.getAscent();
```

```
            // Get the position of the leftmost character in the
               baseline
            xCoordinate = getWidth() / 2 - stringWidth / 2;
            yCoordinate = getHeight() / 2 + stringAscent / 2;
          }

          g.drawString(message, xCoordinate, yCoordinate);
        }

        /** Move the message left */
        public void moveLeft() {
          xCoordinate -= interval;
        }

        /** Move the message right */
        public void moveRight() {
          xCoordinate += interval;
        }

        /** Move the message up */
        public void moveUp() {
          yCoordinate -= interval;
        }

        /** Move the message down */
        public void moveDown() {
          yCoordinate -= interval;
        }

        /** Override get method for preferredSize */
        public Dimension getPreferredSize() {
          return new Dimension(200, 20);
        }

        /** Override get method for minimumSize */
        public Dimension getMinimumSize() {
          return new Dimension(200, 20);
        }
      }
```

Suppose MessagePanel.java was created in the tutorial.jpx project. Compile it. To install the **MessagePanel** bean to the component palette, follow the steps below.

1. Choose *Tools, Configure Palette* or right-click anywhere in the component palette and choose *Properties*. The Palette Properties dialog box appears, as shown in Figure 9.22.
2. Select the Pages tab and choose the page on the component palette on which you want the component to appear. Optionally, you may create a new page by clicking the *Add* button and entering the page name in the Add Page dialog box.
3. Suppose you want to add the **MessagePanel** bean to the *Other* group. Select *Other* in the pages column and click the *Add components* tab to display the dialog box for adding components, as shown in Figure 9.23.

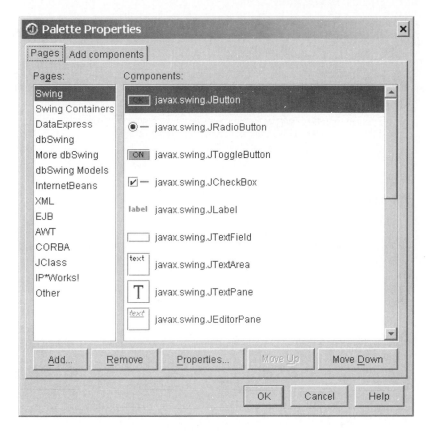

Figure 9.22 *The Palette Property dialog box lets you add beans to the component palette.*

4. You have to select a library that contains the component to be installed. Since MessagePanel is not in any library, you have to first create a library to contain MessagePanel. Click *Select library* to display the Select a different library dialog box, as shown in Figure 9.24.

5. Click *New* in the Select a different library dialog box to display the New Library wizard, as shown in Figure 9.25. Enter the new library name (e.g., `tutorial`) in the Name field, and add the library path in the Library paths section.

6. Click *OK* to add the library. The library appears under the User Home node in the Select a different library dialog box, as shown in Figure 9.26. Select tutorial in the Select a different library dialog box, and click *OK* to return to the Palette Properties dialog box.

7. Check the option *No filtering* and Click *Add from selected library* in the Palette Properties dialog (see Figure 9.27) to display the Browse for class dialog box, as shown in Figure 9.28.

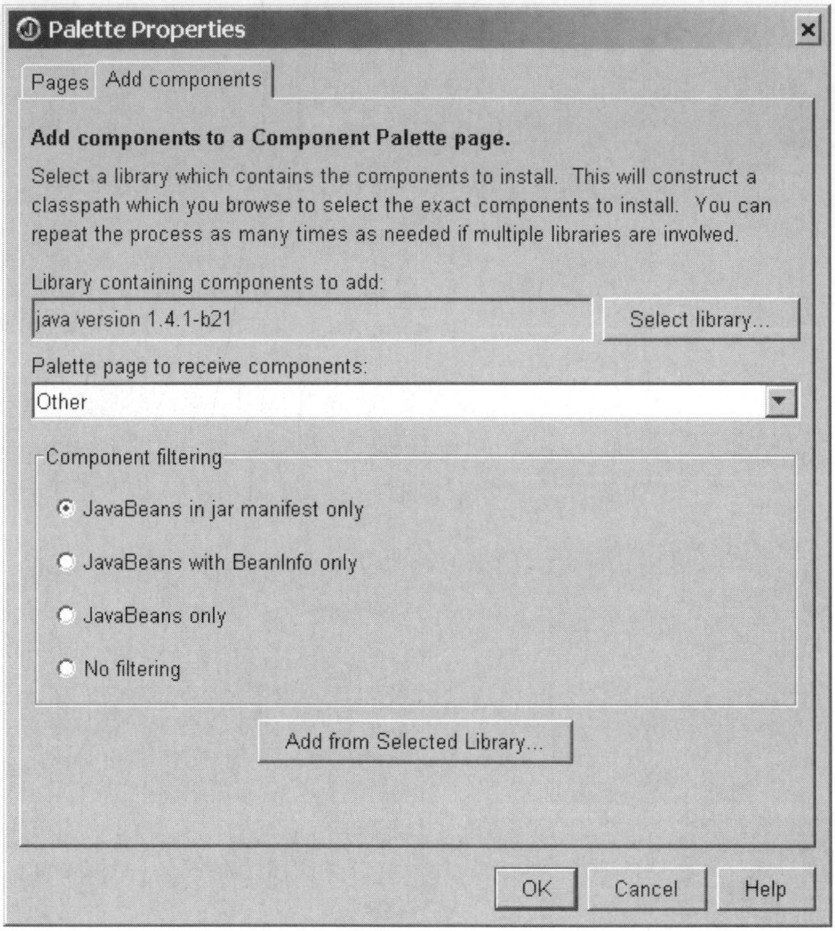

Figure 9.23 *You can select a library that contains the component and specify the filtering options in the Palette Properties dialog box.*

8. Locate **MessagePanel** in the tutorial package. Click *OK* in the Browse for class dialog box to display a dialog box, as shown in Figure 9.29. Click *OK* in this dialog box to confirm it. Click *OK* in the Palette Properties dialog box in Figure 9.27 to close this dialog box.

9.3.2 Using Custom Components

The custom components can be used just like the preintalled components. To test them, create a Java applet named **TestMessagePanel** using the Applet wizard. With TestMessagePanel.java selected in the project pane, choose the Design tab to switch to the UI designer. Click-and-drop MessagePanel from the Other tab in the component palette to the applet, as shown in Figure 9.30.

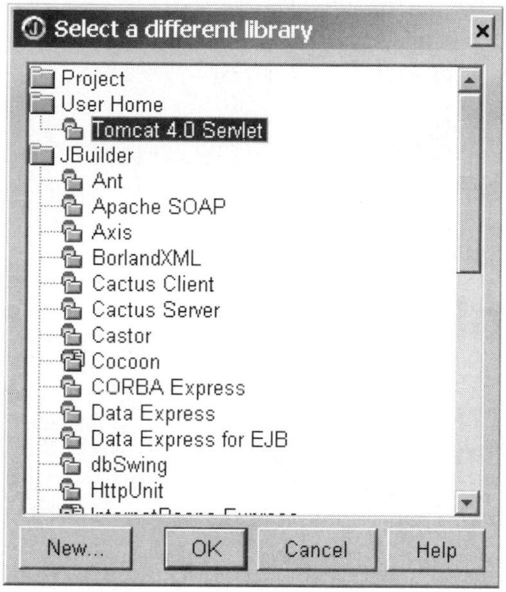

Figure 9.24   *You can select or create a new library from the Select a different library dialog box.*

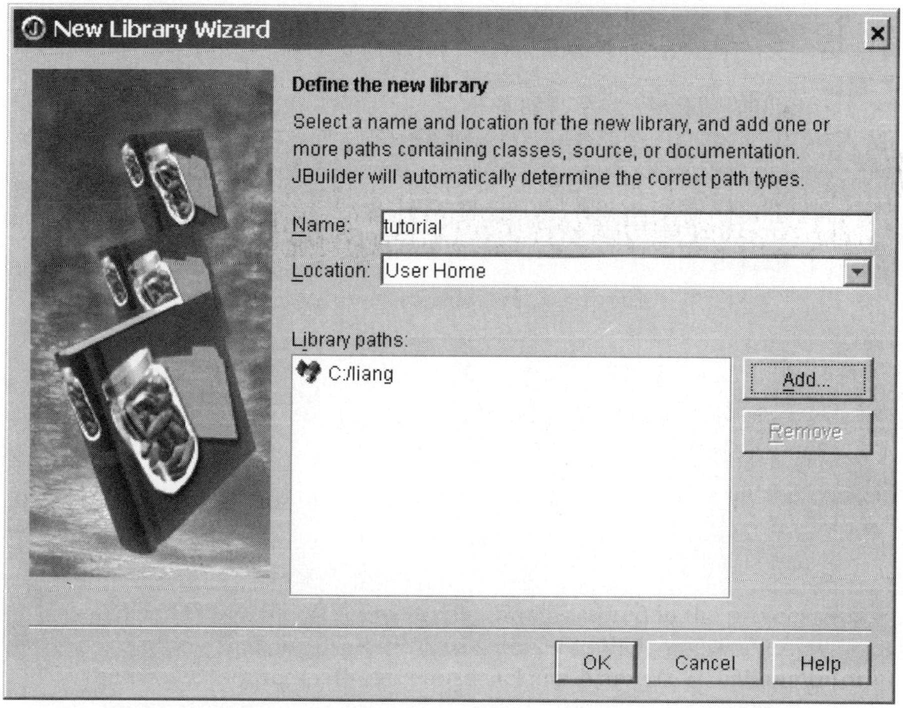

Figure 9.25   *You can create a new library in the New Library wizard.*

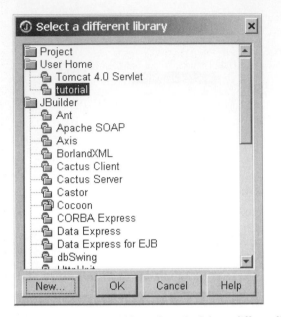

Figure 9.26 *You can select or create a new library from the Select a different library dialog box.*

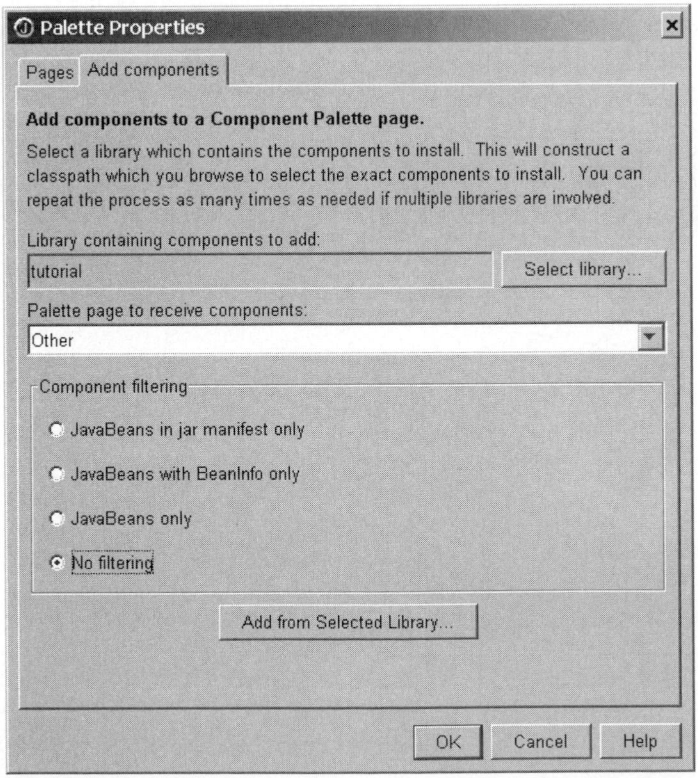

Figure 9.27 *The tutorial library contains the **MessagePanel** component.*

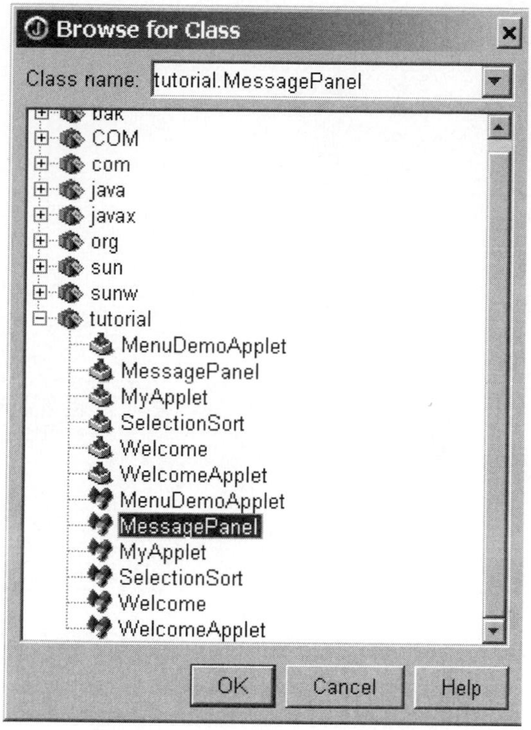

Figure 9.28   *Select the component from the Browse for Class dialog box to install in the component palette.*

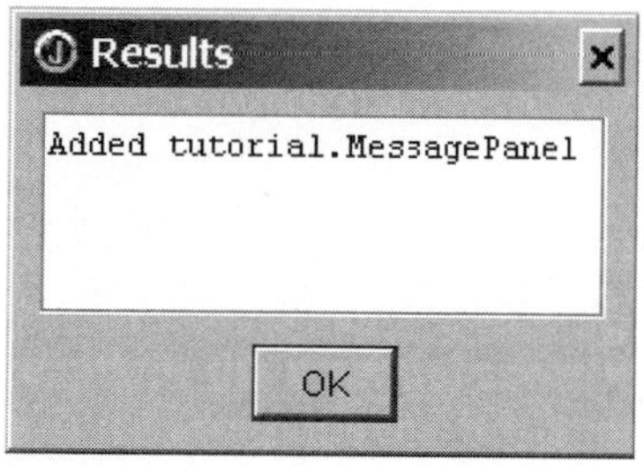

Figure 9.29   *Confirm that the component is to be installed.*

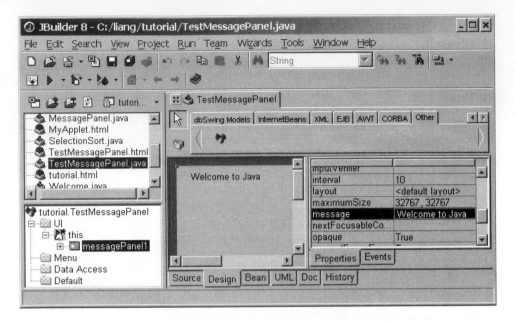

Figure 9.30 *TestMessagePanel.java is created to test the* **MessagePanel** *bean.*

CHAPTER 10

Generating and Viewing javadoc in JBuilder

You can view the javadoc documentation in JBuilder. To do so, you have to first generate the javadoc documentation using the javadoc wizard. This chapter demonstrates how to generate and view javadoc documentation in JBuilder.

> *Note*: The javadoc wizard is a feature of JBuilder Standard and Enterprise.

10.1 Generating javadoc Documentation

Let us use WelcomeApplet.java as example to demonstrate how to generate javadoc using the javadoc wizard. WelcomeApplet.java was created in Chapter 4, "Creating and Testing Java Applets." Change the line comments before each method (e.g., `//Get a parameter value`) to the javadoc comments (e.g., `/** Get a parameter value */`), as shown in Figure 10.1.

Here are the steps to generate the javadoc documentation for Welcome Applet.java.

1. Verify the documentation path. In the Paths tab of the Project Properties dialog box, click the Documentation tab to find the doc path. The Documentation path is c:/liang/doc, as shown in Figure 10.2.
2. Make sure that the **doc** folder is in **liang**. If not, create it.
3. Choose *Wizard*, *Javadoc* to display Javadoc Wizard—Step 1 of 4, as shown in Figure 10.3. You can select JDK 1.1 doclet to format the javadoc documents in JDK 1.1 format, or standard doclet to format the javadoc documents in Java 2 format.
4. Click *Next* to display Javadoc Wizard—Step 2 of 4, as shown in Figure 10.4. You can specify build options in this step.
5. Click *Next* to display Javadoc Wizard—Step 3 of 4, as shown in Figure 10.5. You can select the entire project or a package and specify the lowest visibility to document in this page.

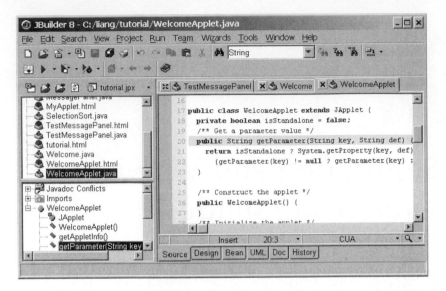

Figure 10.1   *The line comment before each method in WelcomeApplet.java is changed to a javadoc comment.*

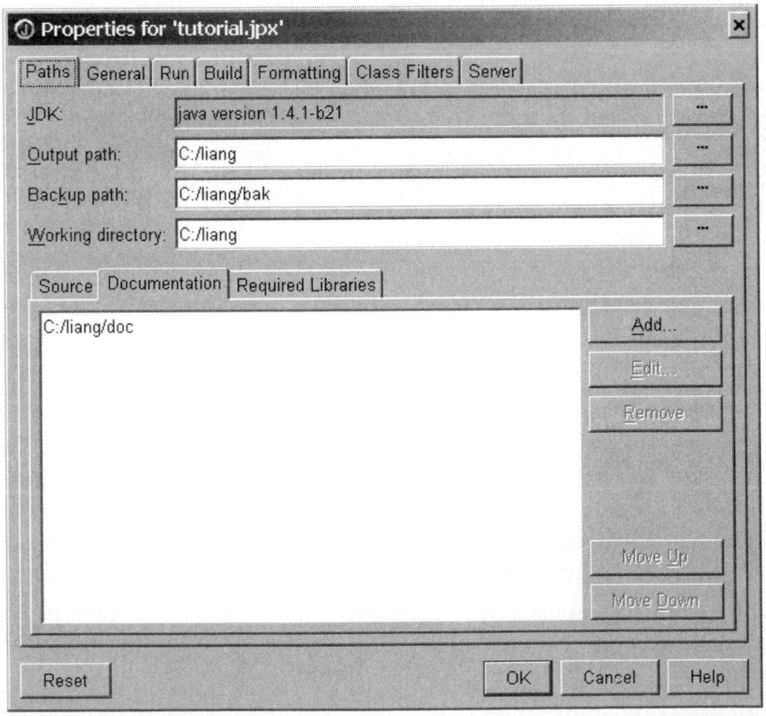

Figure 10.2   *The Document path specifies where the javadoc documentation is stored.*

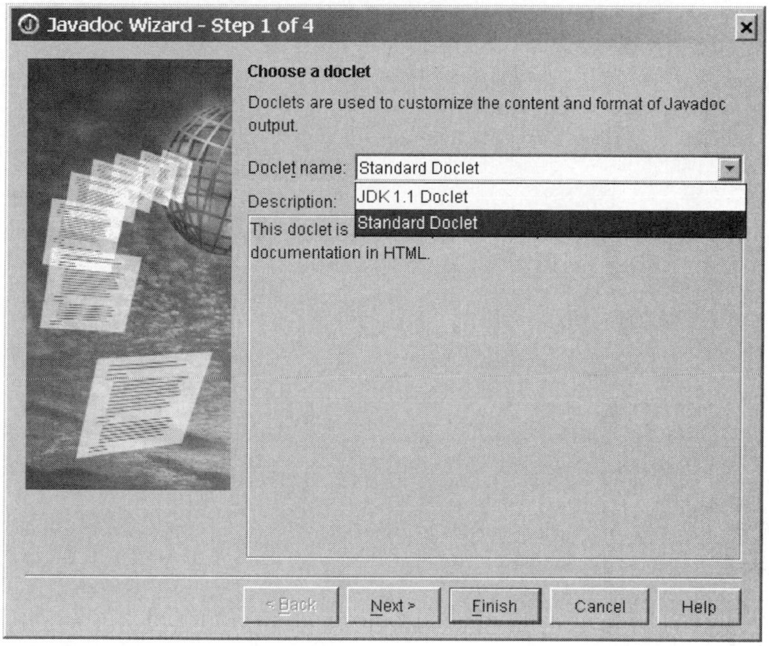

Figure 10.3   *Javadoc Wizard—Step 1 of 4 enables you to select the javadoc format.*

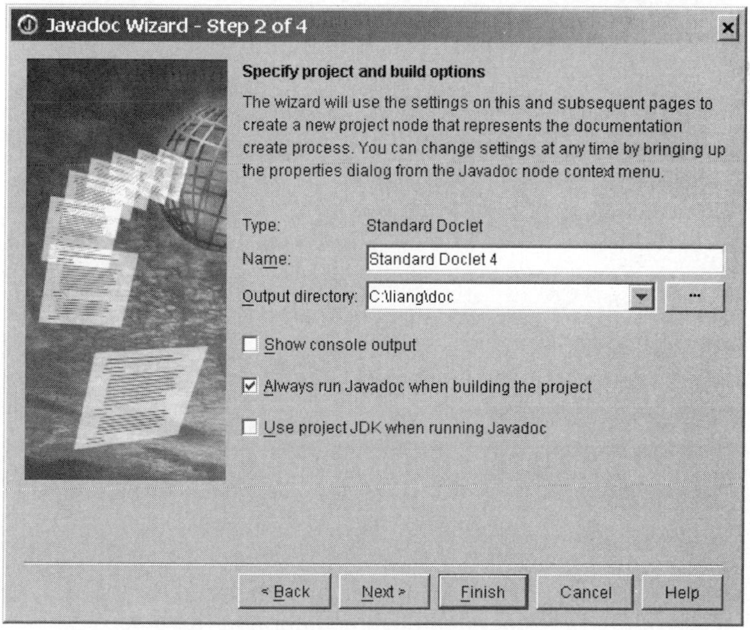

Figure 10.4   *Javadoc Wizard—Step 2 of 4 enables you to specify build options.*

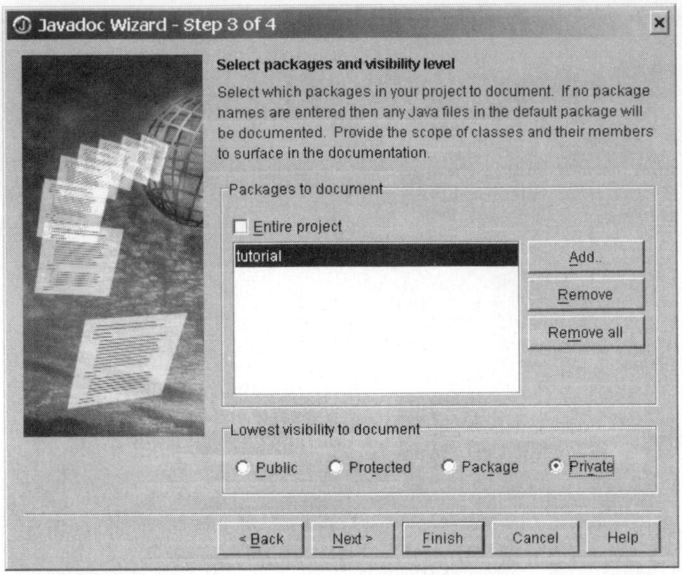

Figure 10.5   *Javadoc Wizard—Step 3 of 4 enables you to specify which package to document and the lowest visibility of the classes and their members to document.*

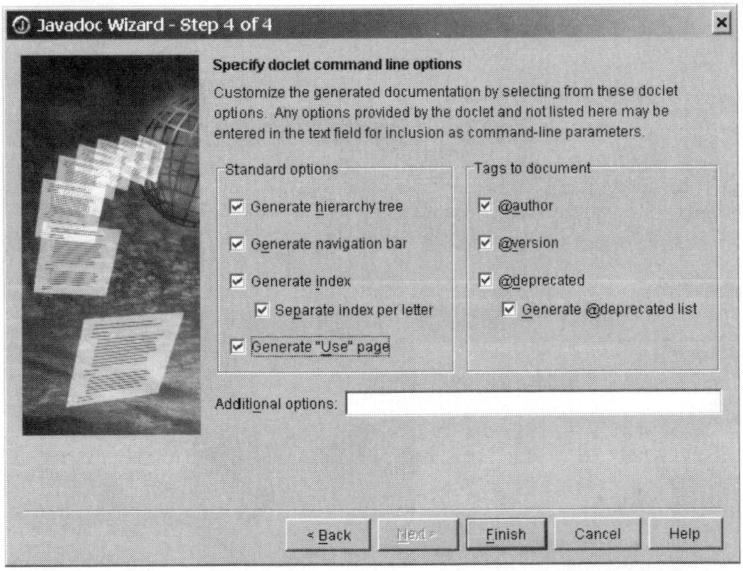

Figure 10.6   *Javadoc Wizard—Step 4 of 4 enables you to customize the generated documentation by selecting the doclet options.*

6. Click *Next* to display Javadoc Wizard—Step 4 of 4, as shown in Figure 10.6. You can customize the generated documentation in this step.

7. Click *Finish* to generate the documentation.

10.2   Viewing Generated javadoc documentation

To view the generated javadoc documentation for a class, choose the Doc tab in the content pane of the class, as shown in Figure 10.7.

You can also view the documentation for the package by choosing the package in the project pane, as shown in Figure 10.8.

Figure 10.7   *You can view the documentation in the content pane.*

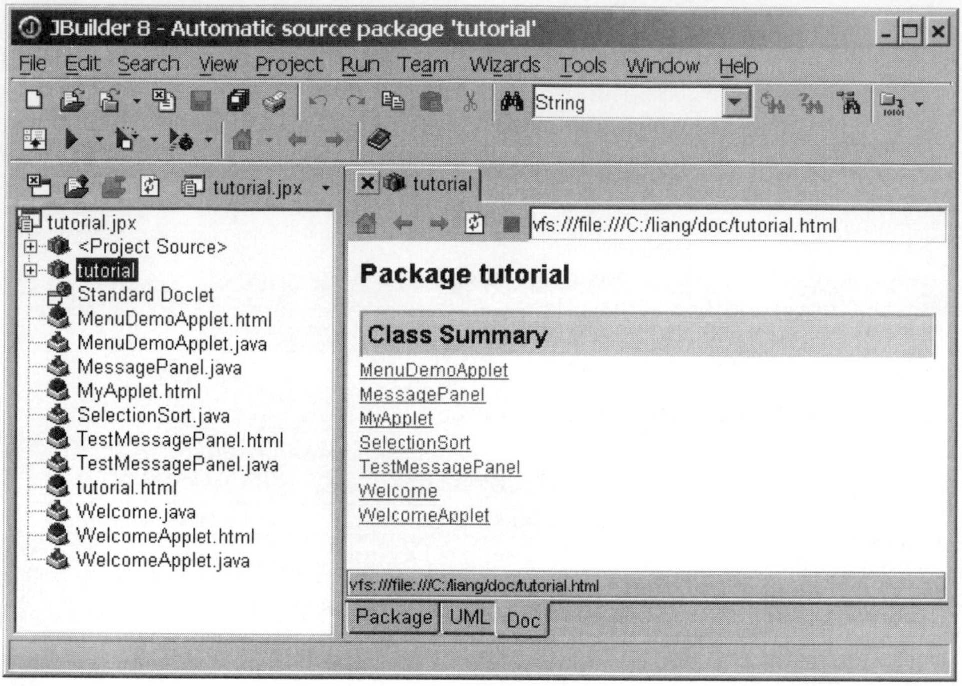

Figure 10.8   *You can view the documentation for the package by choosing the package node in the project pane.*

C H A P T E R   1 1

Packaging and Deploying Java Projects in JBuilder

This chapter introduces the use of JBuilder's Archive Builder wizard to package JBuilder files for deployment. You will also learn how to create shortcuts for applications on Windows.

> *Note:* The Archive wizard is a feature of JBuilder Standard and Enterprise.

11.1   Java Archiving

Your project may consist of many classes and supporting files, such as image files and audio files. All of these files have to be provided to the end-users if your programs are to run on their side. For convenience, Java supports an archive file that can group all the project files in a compressed file.

The Java archive file format (JAR) is based on the popular ZIP file format. JAR can be used as a general archiving tool, but transporting Java applications, applets, and their requisite components (.class files, images, and sounds) in a single file was the primary motivation for its development.

This single file can be deployed on an end-user's machine as an application. It can also be downloaded to a browser in a single HTTP transaction, rather than opening a new connection for each piece. This greatly simplifies application deployment and improves the speed with which an applet can be loaded onto a Web page and begin functioning. The JAR format supports compression, which reduces the size of the file and improves download time still further. Additionally, individual entries in a JAR file can be digitally signed by the applet author to authenticate their origin.

You can create an archive file using the JDK **jar** command or the JBuilder Archive Builder wizard. The following command creates an archive file named WelcomeApplet.jar for classes WelcomeApplet.class:

```
jar -cf WelcomeApplet.jar tutorial/WelcomeApplet.class
```

The **-c** option is for creating a new archive file, and the **-f** option specifies the archive file's name.

11.2   Using the Archive Builder to Package Projects

With the **jar** command, you have to manually identify the dependent files. JBuilder provides Archive Builder, which gathers all the classes on which your program depends into one JAR archive that includes image and audio files.

Let us use the `WelcomeApplet` class in Chapter 4, "Creating and Testing Applets," to demonstrate packaging projects. Here are the steps to follow in generating the archive file:

1. Open the tutorial.jpx project. Choose *Wizards*, *Archive Builder* to start Archive Builder, as shown in Figure 11.1.
2. Since WelcomeApplet can run as an application, choose Application as the Archive type. Click *Next* to display Archive Builder – Step 2 of 6, as shown in Figure 11.2. Check *Compress the contents of the archive.* Click the ellipses to display a File dialog to enter a new file name, WelcomeApplet.jar, in the File field.
3. Click *Next* to display Step 3 of 6 of Archive Builder, as shown in Figure 11.3. Check *Specified only* in the Classes section and the Resources section. Click Add Classes to display the Select a Class dialog box to select Tutorial.WelcomeApplet.

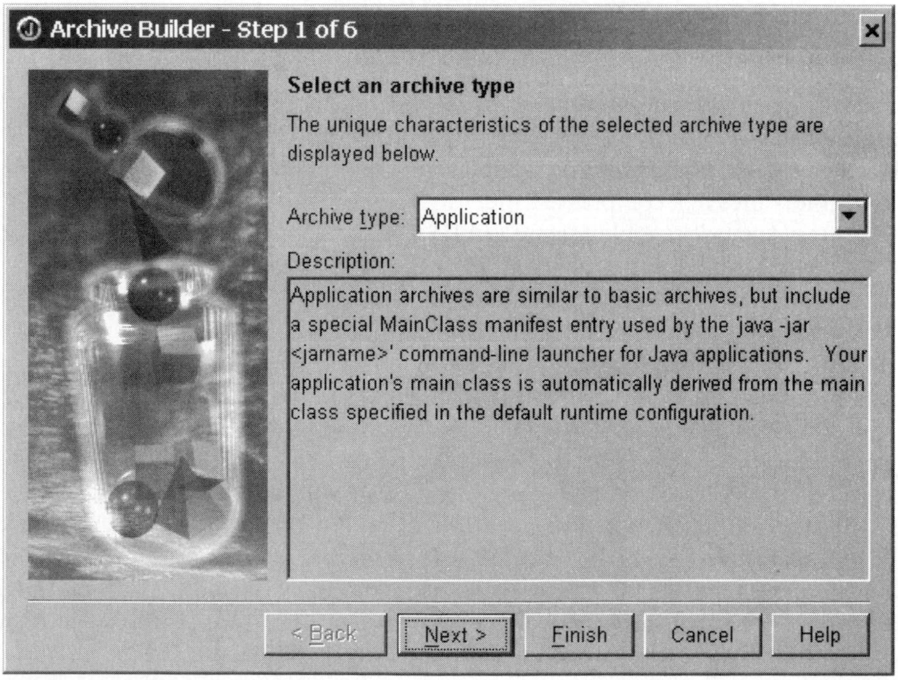

Figure 11.1   *You can use the Archive Builder wizard to create an archive file for the project.*

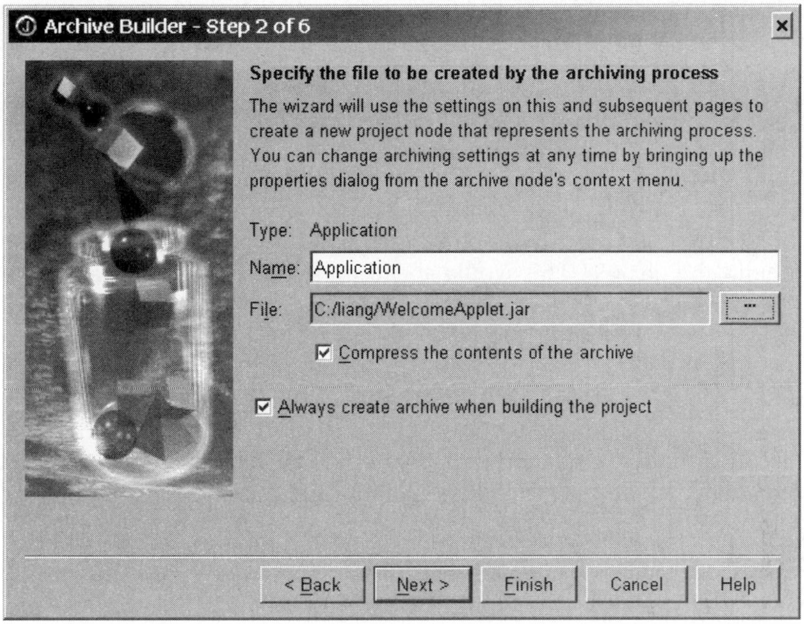

Figure 11.2   *You specify an archive file in Step 2 of Archive Builder.*

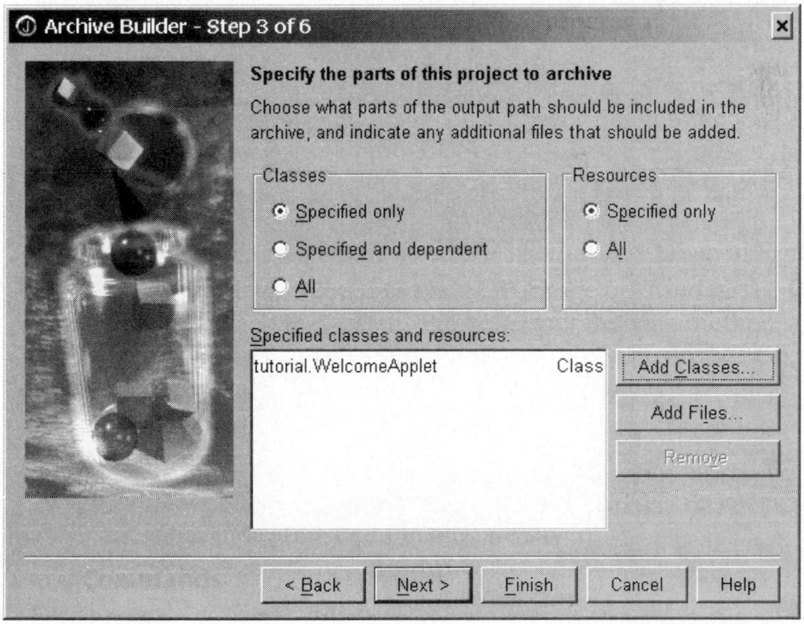

Figure 11.3   *You specify the parts of the project to archive in Step 3 of Archive Builder.*

Click *Next* continually to skip Steps 4 and 5. In Step 6 of 6 of Archive Builder, as shown in Figure 11.4, check *Use the class specified below*. Click the ellipses to display the Select Main Class for the Archive dialog box to select tutorial.WelcomeApplet.

4. Click *Finish* to close the Archive Builder. Rebuild the project to create the archive file. You can see WelcomeApplet.jar in the project pane and its manifest file in the content pane, as shown in Figure 11.5.

> *Tip*: Remove the Application node from the project pane if you don't need to rebuild the .jar file. This would speed up the Rebuild command for building the project.

11.2.1 The Manifest File

As shown in Figure 11.5, a manifest file was created. The manifest is a special file that contains information about the files packaged in a JAR file. For instance, the manifest file in Figure 11.5 contains the following information:

```
Manifest-Version: 1.0
Main-Class: tutorial.WelcomeApplet
```

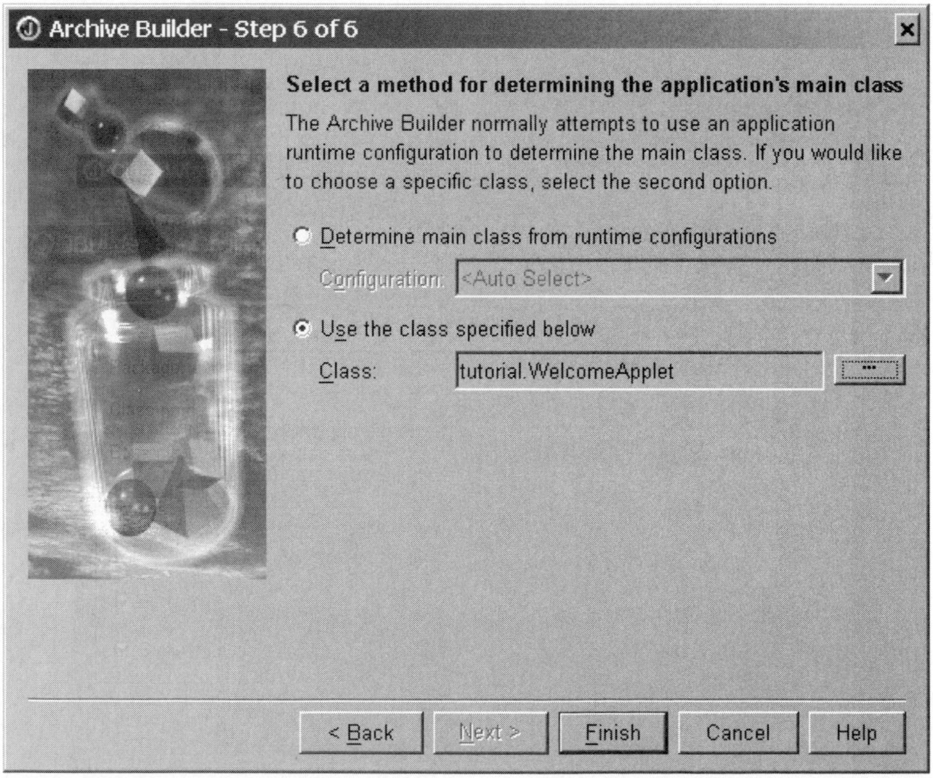

Figure 11.4   *You specify the main method for the archive file in Step 6 of Archive Builder.*

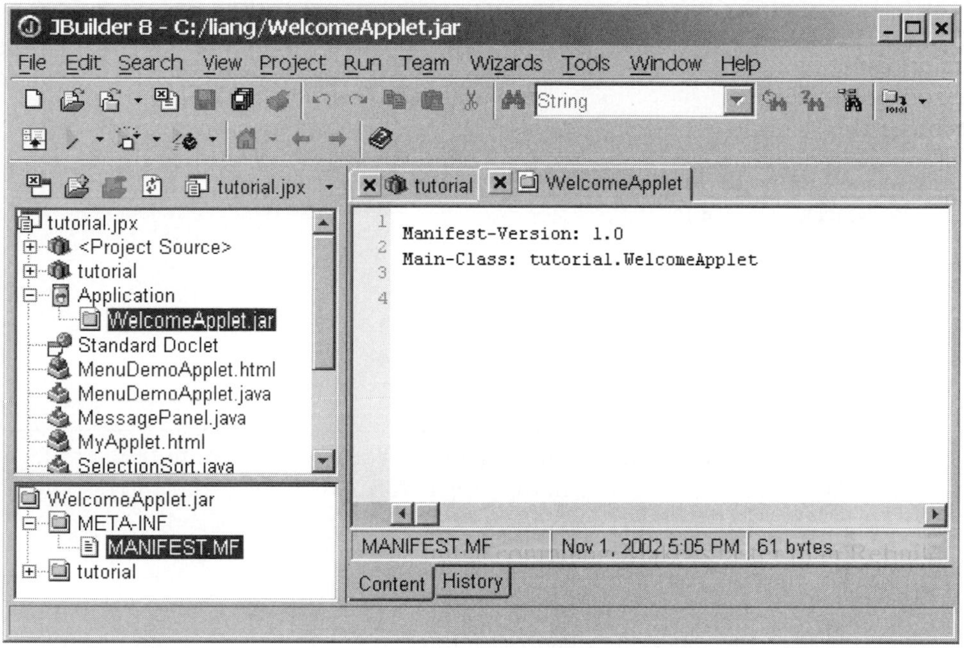

Figure 11.5   *You can view the .jar file and its content in the AppBrowser.*

The Main-Class line specifies that the jar file contains a Java application whose main class is tutorial.WelcomeApplet.

11.2.2   Running Archived Projects

The Archive Builder packages all the class files and dependent resource files into an archive file that can be distributed to the end-user. If the project is a Java application, the user should have a Java Runtime Environment already installed. If it is not installed, the user can download the Java Runtime Environment (JRE) from JavaSoft at *www.javasoft.com/* and install it.

> *Note*: The Java Runtime Environment is the minimum Java platform for running Java programs. It contains the Java interpreter, Java core classes, and supporting files. The JRE does not contain any of the development tools (such as Applet Viewer or javac) or classes that pertain only to a development environment. JRE is a subset of JDK.

Running Archived Files from Java Applications   To run `WelcomeApplet` as an application, simply type the following command:

```
java -jar WelcomeApplet.jar
```

Running Archived Files from Java Applets   To run `WelcomeApplet` as an applet from an archive file that contains the applet, use the ARCHIVE attribute in the HTML file. For example, the HTML file for running the `WelcomeApplet` can be modified as follows:

```
<APPLET
  CODE      = "tutorial.WelcomeApplet.class"
  ARCHIVE   = "WelcomeApplet.jar"
  WIDTH     = 400
  HEIGHT    = 100
  HSPACE    = 0
  VSPACE    = 0
  ALIGN     = Middle
>
</APPLET>
```

> *Note*: If your Java source code is changed, you need to update the .jar file. To update the .jar file, right-click the project file in the project pane to display the context menu, and choose *Rebuild*.

11.3   Create Shortcuts for Java Applications on Windows

You can create an icon on Windows Desktop that the end-user can double-click to start the program. Here are the steps in making a shortcut to run a Java program:

1. Right-click on the desktop and choose *New*, *Shortcut* to display the Create Shortcut wizard, as shown in Figure 11.6.

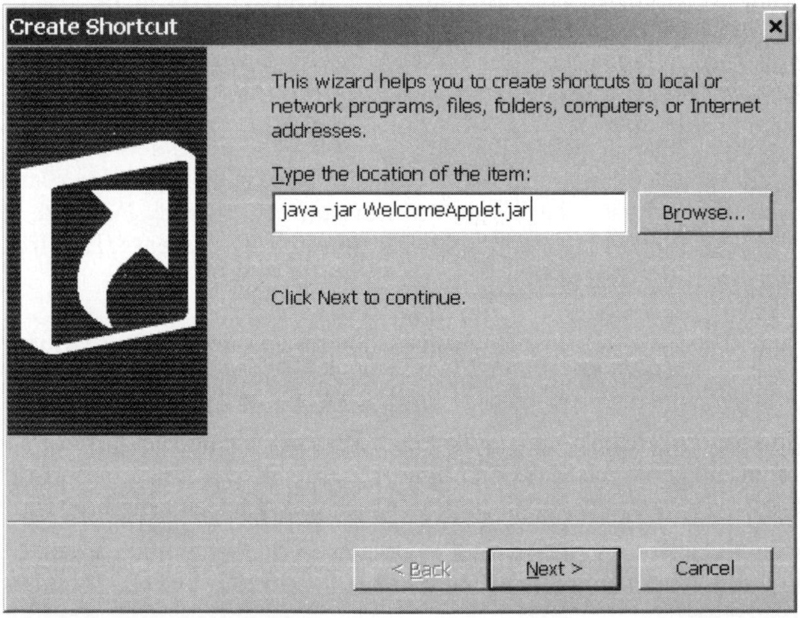

Figure 11.6   *The Create Shortcut wizard helps to create a Windows shortcut.*

2. Type **java -jar WelcomeApplet.jar** in the text box, as shown in Figure 11.6. Click *Next* to display the dialog box, as shown in Figure 11.7.

3. Type **WelcomeApplet** as the name for the shortcut in Figure 11.7, and click *Finish* to create the shortcut, as shown in Figure 11.8.

4. Right-click the WelcomeApplet shortcut you just created and select Properties to display the WelcomeApplet Properties dialog box, as shown in Figure 11.9.

5. Type **c:\liang** in the Start in field. This folder contains WelcomeApplet.jar. Click *OK* to close the WelcomeApplet Properties dialog box. You can now double-click WelcomeApplet on the desktop to run the WelcomeApplet application.

6. (Optional) You can set a custom icon for the application by clicking the Change Icon button in the WelcomeApplet Properties dialog box.

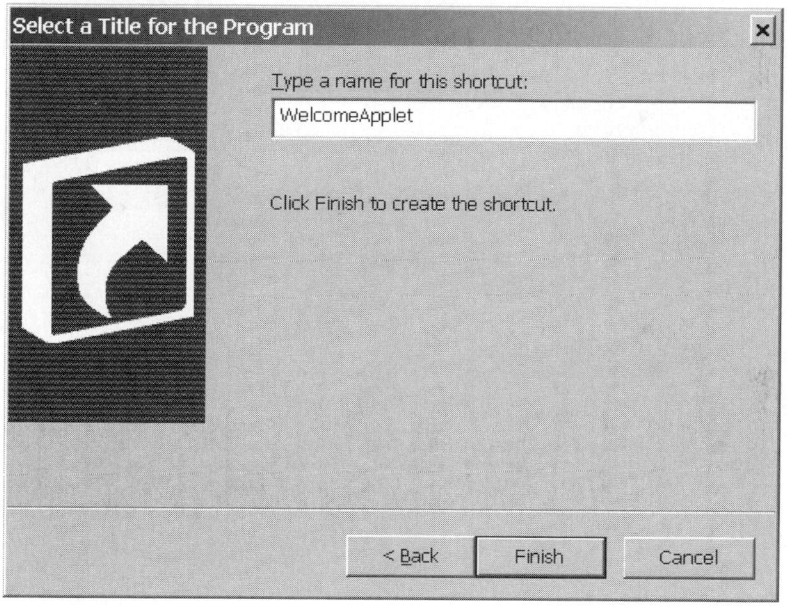

Figure 11.7   *Select an appropriate name for the shortcut.*

Figure 11.8   *The WelcomeApplet shortcut is created on the Windows desktop.*

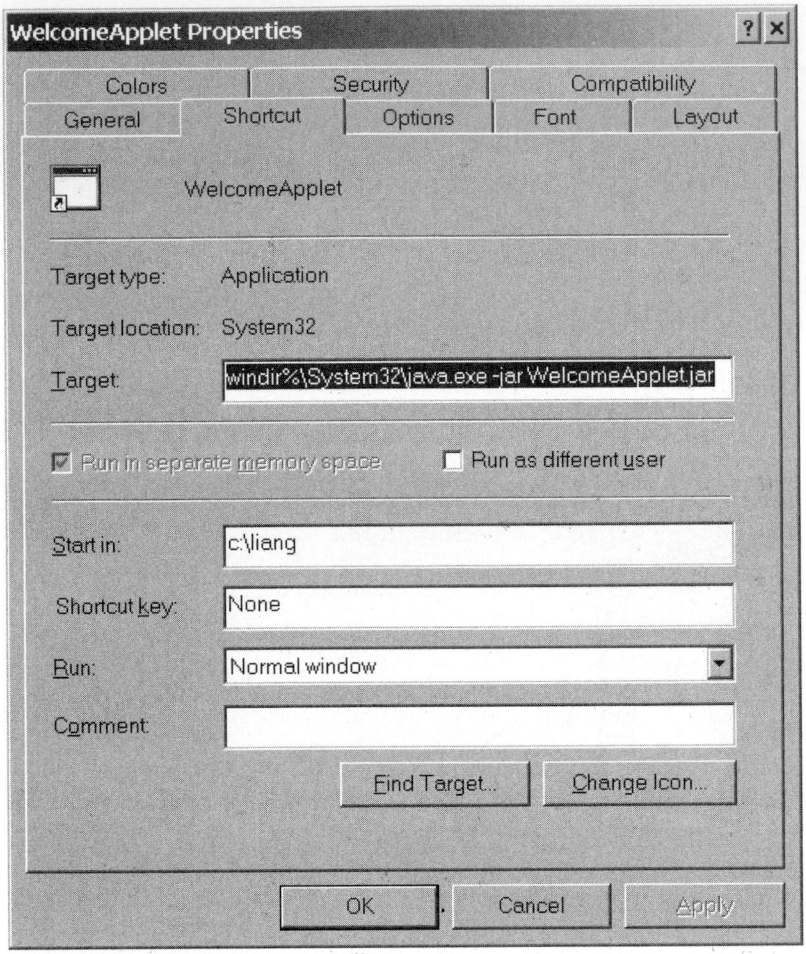

WelcomeApplet Properties ? ✕

| Colors | Security | Compatibility |

| General | Shortcut | Options | Font | Layout |

WelcomeApplet

Target type: Application

Target location: System32

Target: %windir%\System32\java.exe -jar WelcomeApplet.jar

☑ Run in separate memory space ☐ Run as different user

Start in: c:\liang

Shortcut key: None

Run: Normal window ▾

Comment:

Find Target... Change Icon...

OK Cancel Apply

Figure 11.9 *Select an appropriate name for the shortcut.*

C H A P T E R   1 2

Creating and Running Servlets and JSP from JBuilder

To run Java servlets and JavaServer pages, you need a servlet engine. Many servlet engines are available. *Tomcat*, developed by Apache (*www.apache.org*), is a standard reference implementation for Java servlet 2.2 and Java Server Pages 1.1. It is free. It can be used standalone as a Web server or be plugged into a Web server like Apache, Netscape Enterprise Server, or Microsoft Internet Information Server. Tomcat has been integrated with JBuilder Enterprise Edition. This chapter demonstrates how to create and run a Java Servlet and JSP from JBuilder.

12.1   Creating a Servlet

Here are the steps to create a servlet in JBuilder:

1. Create a new project to hold files for the servlet, as follows:
   1.1. Choose *File, New Project* to display the Project wizard, as shown in Figure 12.1. Type `servletjspdemo` in the Name field and `c:/liangservletjsp` in the Directory field. Click *Next* to display Project Wizard—Step 2 of 3, as shown in Figure 12.2.
   1.2. In Step 2 of the Project wizard, type `c:/liangservletjsp` in the Output path field, `C:/liangservletjsp/bak` in the Backup path field, and `C:/liangservletjsp` in the Working directory field. Change the source path to `C:/liangservletjsp`. Click *Finish* to create the project, as shown in Figure 12.3.
2. In the Web page of the object gallery, click the Servlet icon to display the Servlet wizard, as shown in Figure 12.4.

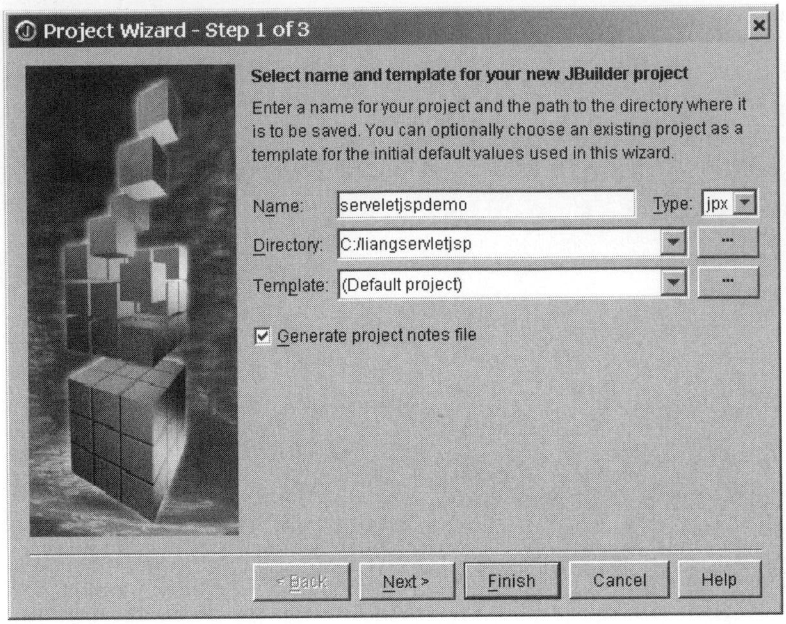

Figure 12.1 *Using the Project wizard to create a new project to hold files for servlets and JSP.*

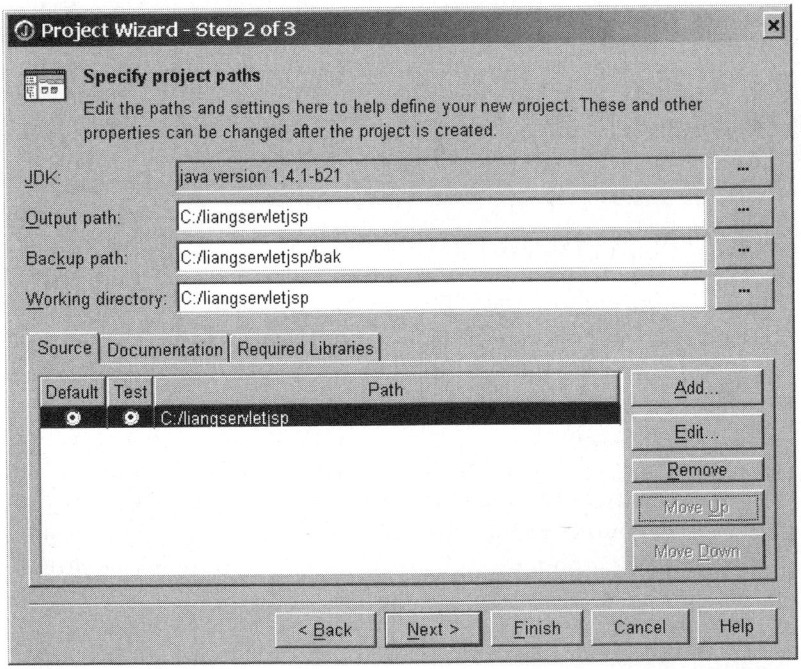

Figure 12.2 *You need to set proper paths for the project in Project Wizard—Step 2 of 3.*

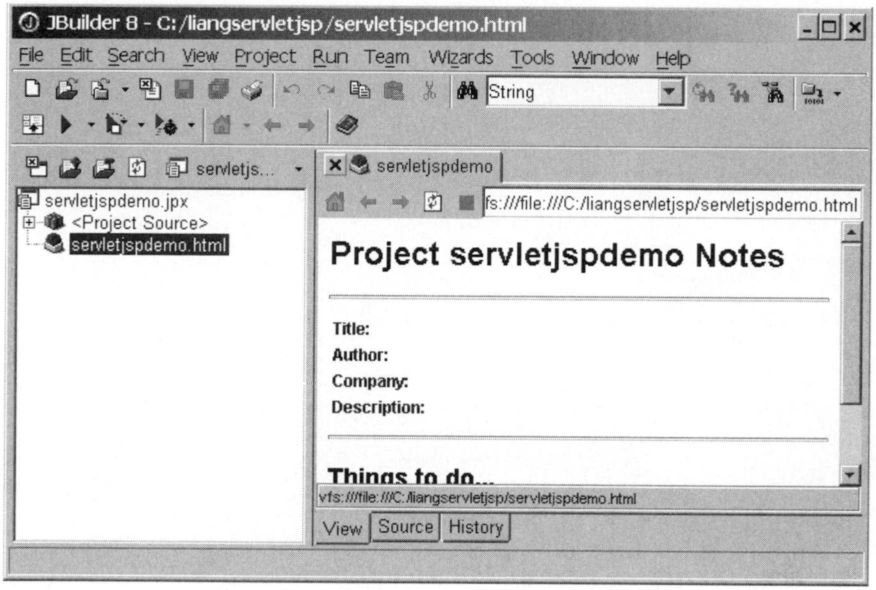

Figure 12.3   *A new project is created.*

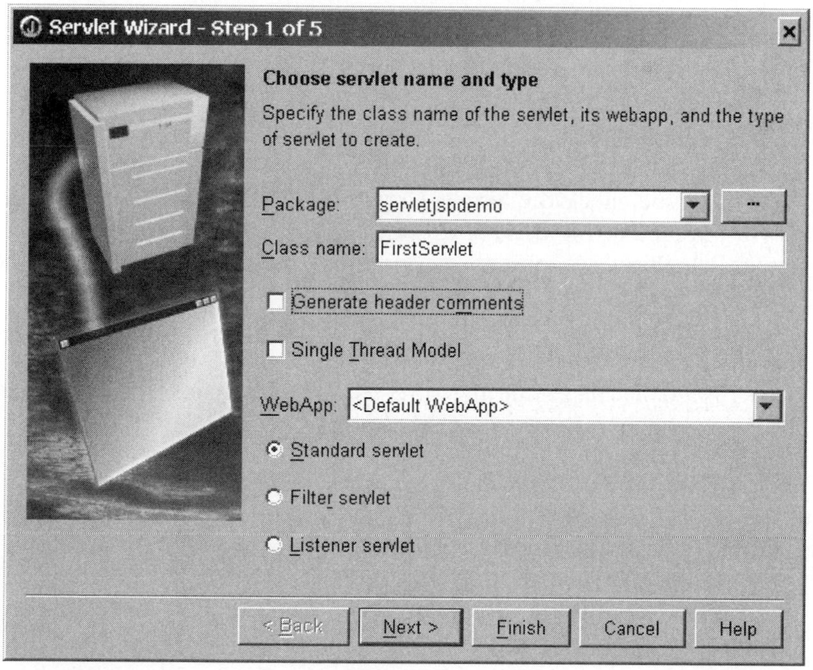

Figure 12.4   *Servlet Wizard—Step 1 of 5 enables you to specify a servlet class.*

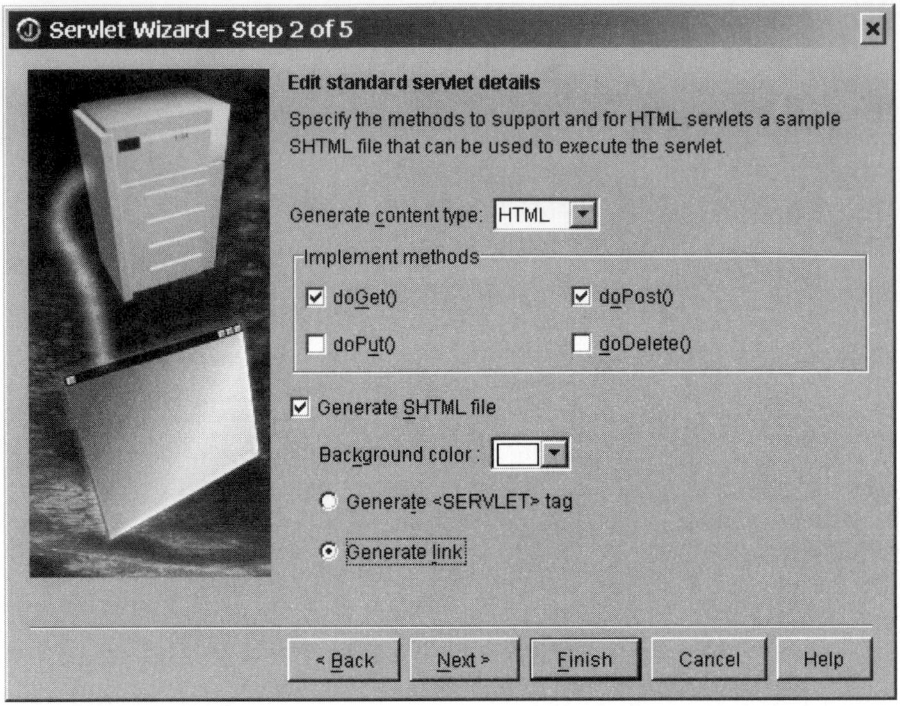

Figure 12.5 *Servlet Wizard—Step 2 of 5 enables you to specify method types.*

3. Type **servletjspdemo** in the Package field and **FirstServlet** in the Class name field. Check *Standard servlet* and click *Next* to display Servlet Wizard—Step 2 of 5, as shown in Figure 12.5.

> *Note*: If you check the Single Thread Model option, the generated servlet will implement the **SingleThreadModel** interface. This is a marker interface, which signifies that the servlet runs in a single thread model. Normally, your servlet runs on multiple threads. Whenever a request arrives, the servlet engine spawns a new thread to handle the request. You have to be careful to ensure that data can be accessed simultaneously. If data might be corrupted because multiple threads access the data simultaneously, you may implement the **SingleThreadModel** interface or synchronize the data in the **doGet** and **goPost** methods.

4. In Servlet Wizard—Step 2 of 5, select *doGet* and *doPost* in the Implement methods section, check Generate SHTML file, and select *Generate link*. Click Next to display Servlet Wizard—Step 3 of 5, as shown in Figure 12.6.

5. Servlet Wizard—Step 3 of 5 enables you to optionally specify a name and mapping for the servlet. Skip it and Click *Next* to display Servlet Wizard—Step 4 of 5, as shown in Figure 12.7.

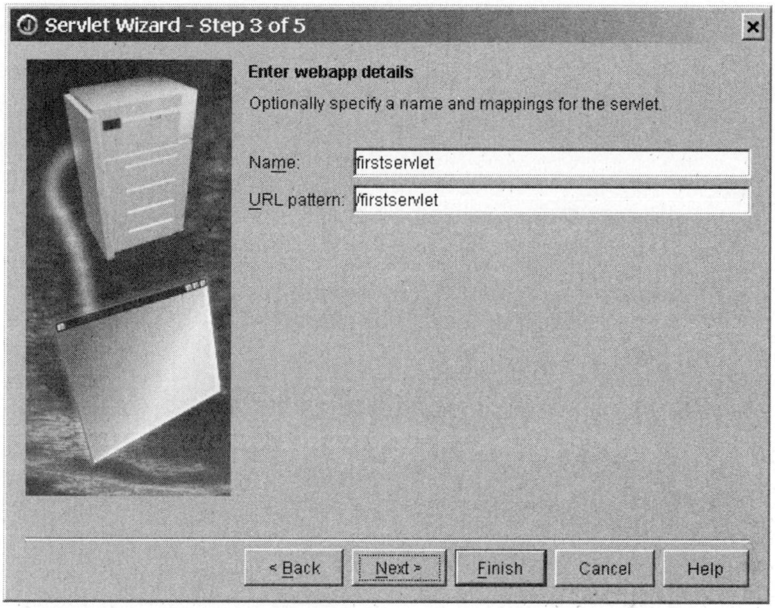

Figure 12.6   *Servlet Wizard—Step 3 of 5 enables you to optionally specify a name and mapping for the servlet.*

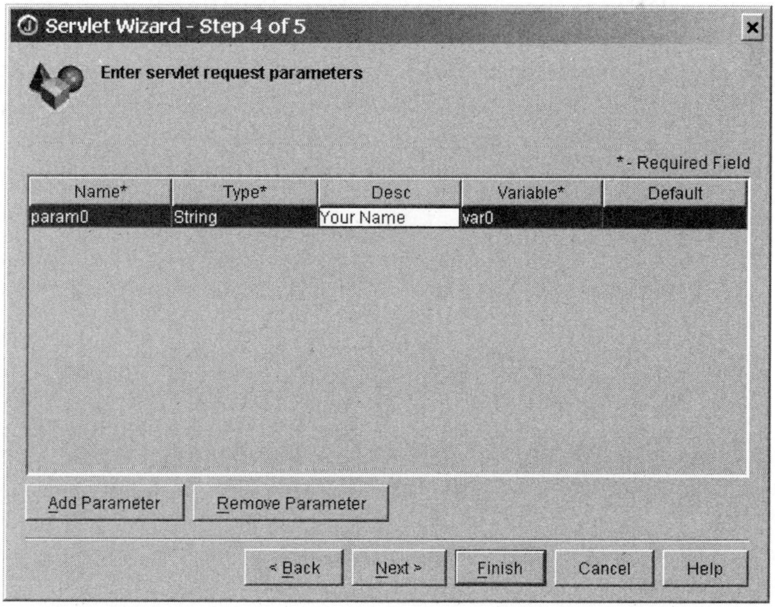

Figure 12.7   *Servlet Wizard—Step 4 of 5 enables you to specify servlet parameters.*

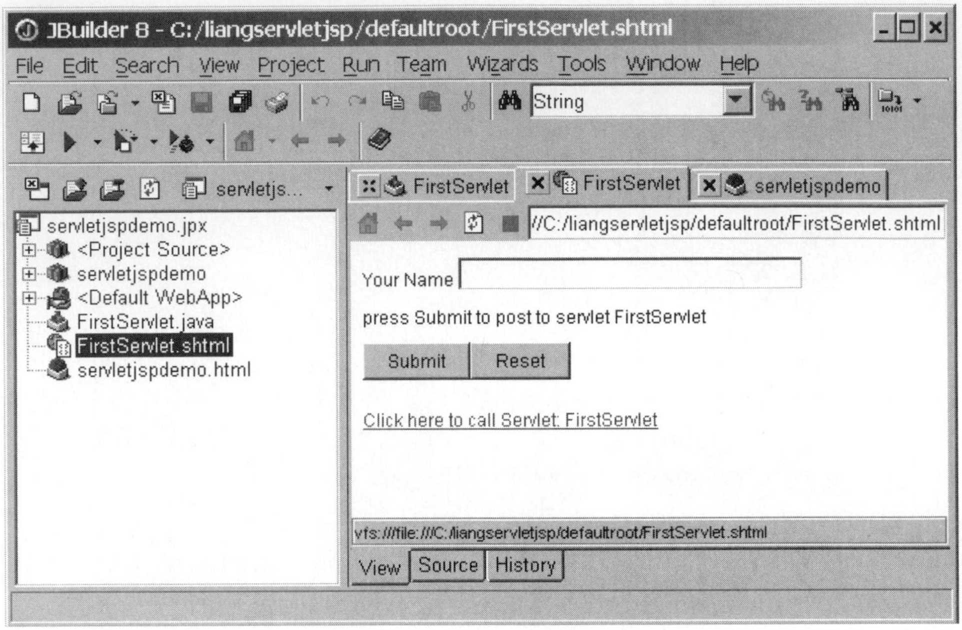

Figure 12.8   *The Servlet wizard generated FirstServlet.java and FirstServlet.shtml.*

6. Type **Your Name** in the Desc field. Click *Finish*. JBuilder generates two files: FirstServlet.java (Listing 12.1) and FirstServlet.shtml (Listing 12.2). First-Servlet.shtml is displayed in Figure 12.8. JBuilder also automatically added a servlet in the Required Libraries for this project, as shown in Figure 12.9.

7. FirstServlet.java contains the source code for the Servlet class **FirstServlet**. In the **doPost** method of this class, add the following statement to send a text string to the browser

```
out.println("<p>Hi, " + var0 + "<p>");
```

before

```
out.println("</body></html>");
```

> *Note*: The SHTML is the same as the HTML file except that the .shtml extension indicates the HTML file for the servlets.

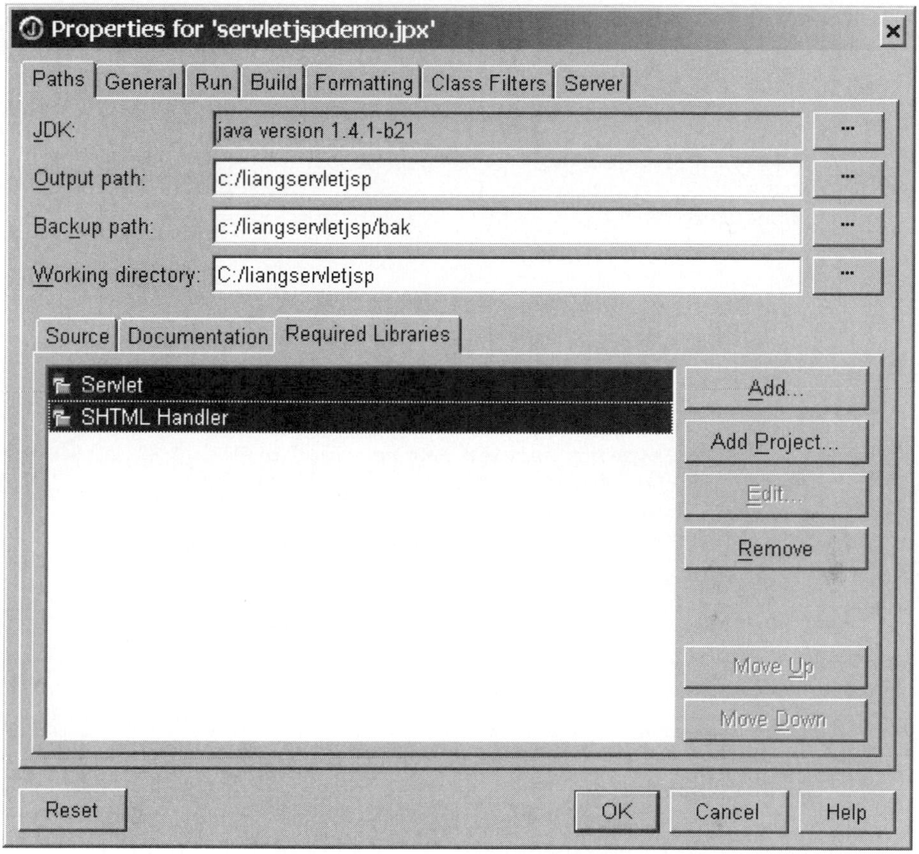

Figure 12.9   *The Servlet library was automatically placed in the project by the Servlet wizard.*

Listing 12.1: FirstServlet.java

```java
package servletjspdemo;

import javax.servlet.*;
import javax.servlet.http.*;
import java.io.*;
import java.util.*;

public class FirstServlet extends HttpServlet {
  private static final String CONTENT_TYPE = "text/html";

  /**Initialize global variables*/
  public void init(ServletConfig config) throws ServletException {
    super.init(config);
  }
```

```
/**Process the HTTP Get request*/
public void doGet(HttpServletRequest request, HttpServletResponse
  response) throws ServletException, IOException {
  String var0 = "";
  try {
    var0 = request.getParameter("param0");
  }
  catch(Exception e) {
    e.printStackTrace();
  }
  response.setContentType(CONTENT_TYPE);
  PrintWriter out = response.getWriter();
  out.println("<html>");
  out.println("<head><title>FirstServlet</title></head>");
  out.println("<body>");
  out.println("<p>The servlet has received a GET. " +
    "This is the reply.</p>");
  out.println("</body></html>");
}

/**Process the HTTP Post request*/
public void doPost(HttpServletRequest request, HttpServletResponse
  response) throws ServletException, IOException {
  String var0 = "";
  try {
    var0 = request.getParameter("param0");
  }
  catch(Exception e) {
    e.printStackTrace();
  }
  response.setContentType(CONTENT_TYPE);
  PrintWriter out = response.getWriter();
  out.println("<html>");
  out.println("<head><title>FirstServlet</title></head>");
  out.println("<body>");
  out.println("<p>The servlet has received a POST. " +
    "This is the reply.</p>");
  out.println("<p>Hi, " + var0 + " <p>"); // Manually added
  out.println("</body></html>");
  out.close(); // Close stream
}

/**Clean up resources*/
public void destroy() {
}
}
```

Listing 12.2: FirstServlet.shtml

```
<html>
<head>
<title>
FirstServlet
</title>
</head>
<body>

<form action="/servlet/servletjspdemo.FirstServlet" method="post">
<p>Your Name <input type="text" name="param0"></p>
<p>press Submit to post to servlet FirstServlet</p>
<p><input type="submit" name="Submit" value="Submit">
<input type="reset" value="Reset"></p>
</form>
<p><a href="/servlet/servletjspdemo.FirstServlet">
  Click here to call Servlet: FirstServlet</a></p>
</body>
</html>
```

12.2 Running the Servlet

Before running the servlet, select Single server for all services and choose Tomcat 4.0 in the Server page of the Project Properties dialog box, as shown in Figure 12.10. Click *OK* to close the dialog box.

To run the servlet, choose FirstServlet.shtml in the project pane, right-click the mouse button to display the context menu. Click *Web Run* using "FirstServlet" from the menu to start the Tomcat server and the servlet, as shown in Figure 12.11. The output from the server appears in the Message page, as shown in Figure 12.12.

By default, Tomcat server starts at port 8080. If this port is in use, JBuilder automatically finds the next available port.

12.3 Testing the Servlet

You can now test the servlet in JBuilder. Type Joe in the Your Name box and click the Submit button, as shown in Figure 12.12. You will see a response from the servlet "Hi, Joe" displayed in the content pane, as shown in Figure 12.13. In Figure 12.13, the View tab renders FirstServlet.shtml, the Source tab displays the source code for FirstServlet.shtml, the Web View tab renders the generated Web contents, and the Web View Source tab displays the source code of the generated Web text file.

You can also test it from the Web browser using the URL *http://localhost:8080/FirstServlet.shtml*, as shown in Figure 12.14. Type Joe in the Your Name box and click the Submit button. You will see a response from the Tomcat server displayed in Figure 12.15.

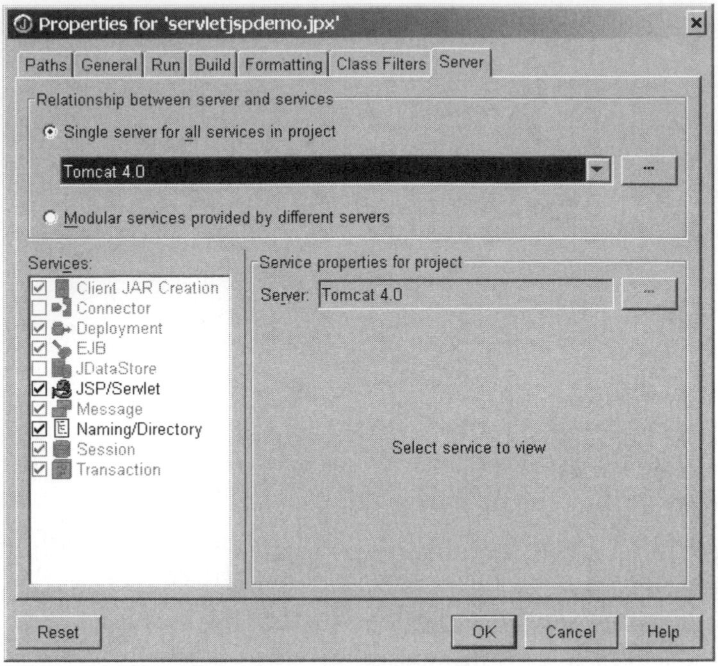

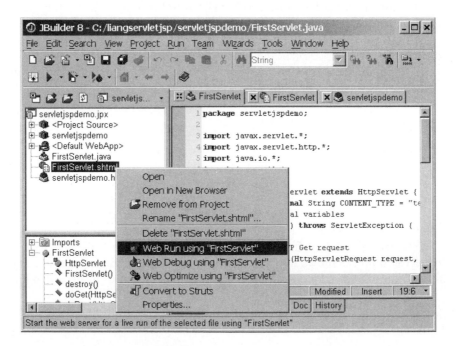

Figure 12.10   *The Server page of the Project Properties dialog box enables you to select a server.*

Figure 12.11   *The servlet can be started from the JBuilder IDE.*

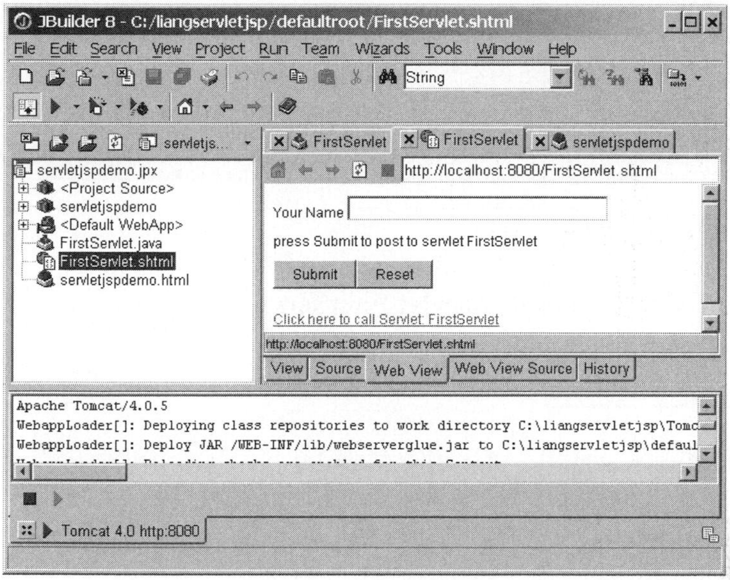

Figure 12.12   *Tomcat server and servlet are started from JBuilder.*

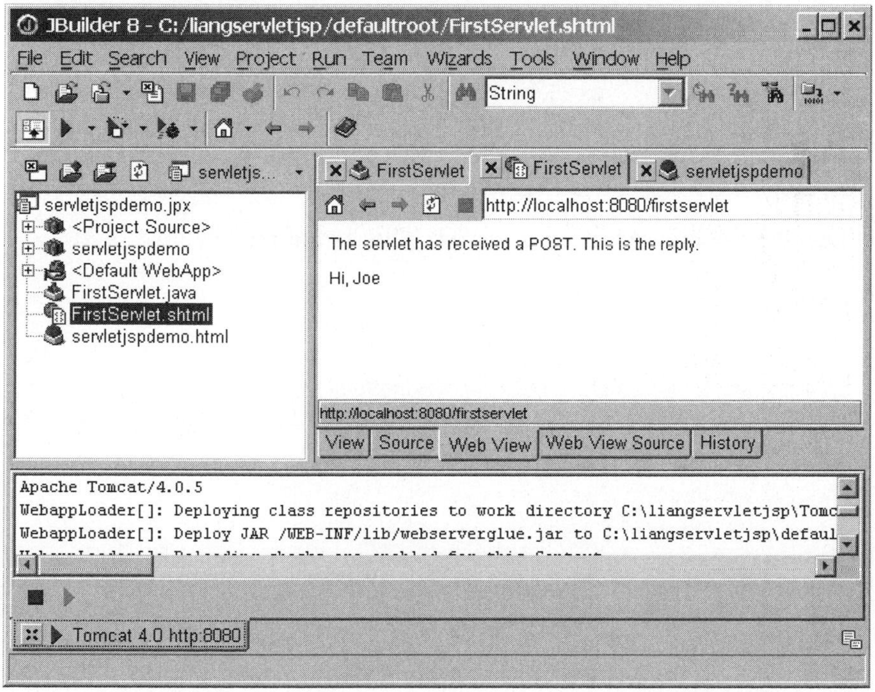

Figure 12.13   *You can test the servlet response from JBuilder.*

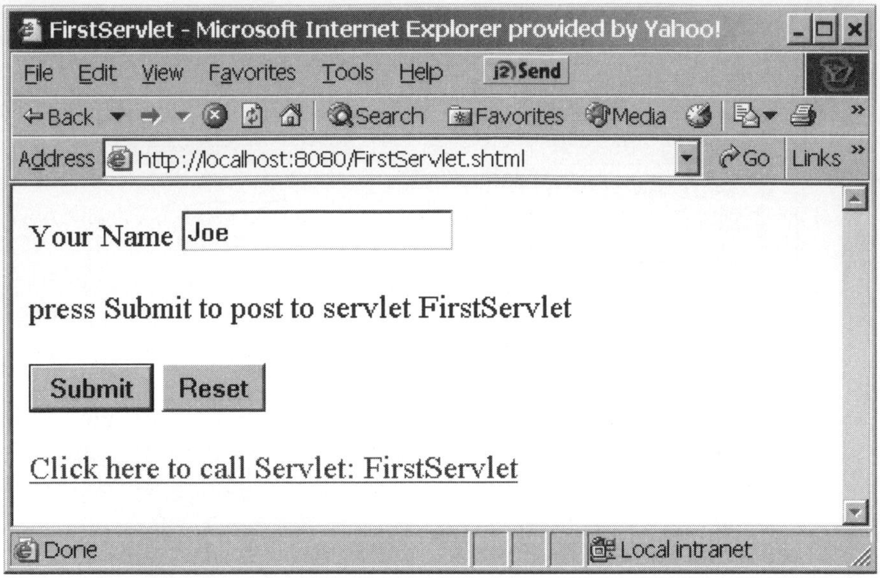

Figure 12.14 *You can test the servlet response from a Web browser.*

Figure 12.15 *The response from the servlet is shown in the Web browser.*

Note: You can use the servlet from anywhere on the Internet if your JBuilder is running on a host machine on the Internet. Suppose the host name is liang.armstrong.edu, use the URL *http://liang.armstrong.edu:8080/FirstServlet.shtml* to test the servlet.

12.4   Creating and Running a JavaServer Page

In this section, you will develop a JavaServer page to display factorials, as shown in Figure 12.16. Here are the steps to create the JSP in JBuilder:

1. Open servletjspdemo.jpx. In the Web page of the object gallery, click the JavaServer Page icon to display the JSP wizard, as shown in Figure 12.17.

2. Type **FirstJSP** in the Name field and uncheck all options. Click *Finish* to generate FirstJSP.jsp.

3. With FirstJSP.jsp selected in the project pane, click the Source tab in the content pane to display the source code for FirstJSP.jsp. Complete the code for FirstJSP.jsp, as shown in Figure 12.18. The complete source code is shown in Listing 12.3.

4. Run FirstJSP.jsp by choosing *Web Run* from the context menu of Factorial.jsp in the project pane. You will see the execution result of Factorial.jsp displayed in the Web View tab in the content pane, as shown in Figure 12.19. You can also run it from a Web browser, as shown in Figure 12.16.

Note: In the context menu of FirstJSP.jsp in the project pane, the Web Run command may be Web Run using "FirstServlet." It is fine to use the same configuration for a servlet. Optionally, you may create a new configuration to run the JSP.

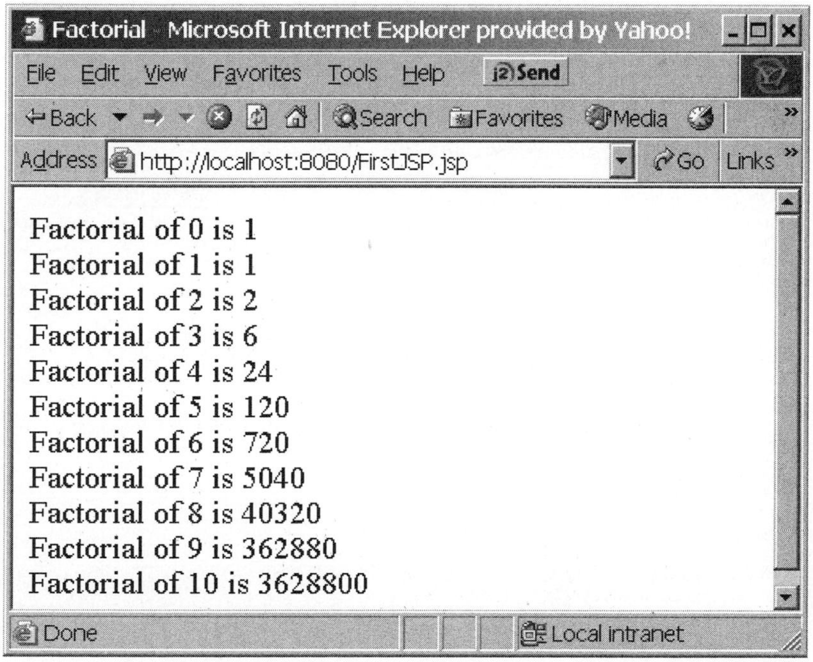

Figure 12.16   *The factorials are displayed in the JavaServer page.*

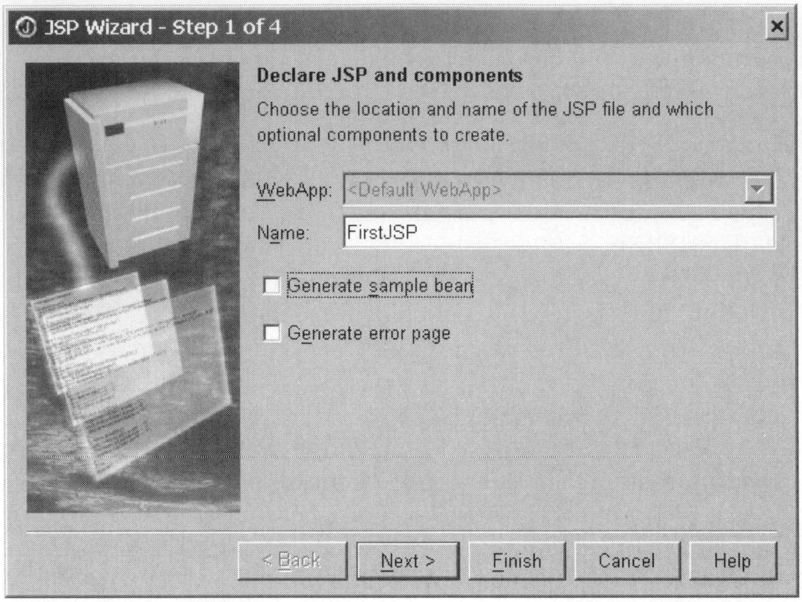

Figure 12.17 *You can create a JavaServer page using the JSP wizard in JBuilder.*

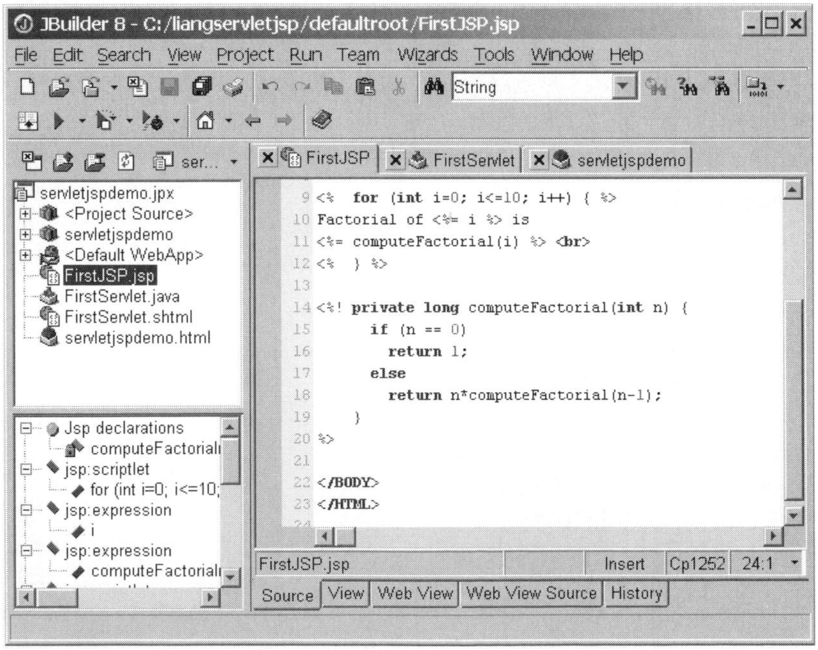

Figure 12.18 *The execution result of the server page is displayed in the JBuilder content pane.*

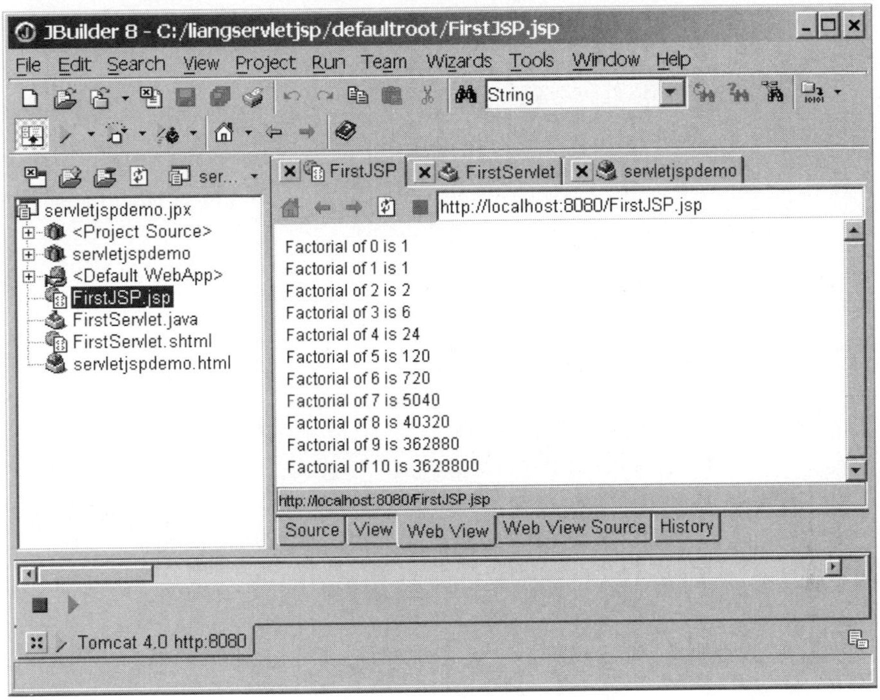

Figure 12.19   *The execution result of the server page is displayed in the JBuilder content pane.*

Listing 12.3 Factorial.jsp

```
<HTML>
<HEAD>
<TITLE>
Factorial
</TITLE>
</HEAD>
<BODY>

<% for (int i=0; i<=10; i++) { %>
Factorial of <%= i %> is
<%= computeFactorial(i) %> <br>
<% } %>

<%! private long computeFactorial(int n) {
    if (n == 0)
      return 1;
    else
      return n*computeFactorial(n-1);
    }
%>

</BODY>
</HTML>
```

JBuilder Frequently Asked Questions

QUESTIONS

1. Why do I have to create a project?
2. How do I create a Java program?
3. How do I compile a Java program?
4. How do I run a Java program?
5. How do I test a Java applet from JBuilder?
6. How do I delete a file from the IDE?
7. How do I delete a .class file from the IDE?
8. How do I add a file or a package to a project?
9. How do I remove a file or a package from a project?
10. How do I rename a file?
11. How do I set the code style to generate the template with the next-line style?
12. How do I set the block indent for the Java source code editor?
13. How do I format the code in JBuilder 7 or higher?
14. How do I change the color and font in the Java source editor?
15. How do I disable code insight?
16. How do I change the look-and-feel to Motif?
17. How do I disable audio sound in the IDE?
18. How do I get help on Java classes, methods, and keywords?
19. How do I view the source code for Java classes in the Java API?
20. How do I search a text in all the source files in the source path?
21. How do I generate Javadoc documents?
22. How do I create an archive file in JBuilder?
23. How do I add a database driver in JBuilder?
24. How do I enable or disable source package discovery and compilation?
25. I tried to run the program from the DOS prompt but got `java.lang.NoClassDef` `FoundError` exception. What is wrong?
26. I tried to run the program from the DOS prompt but got `java.lang.NoSuch` `MethodFoundError` exception. What is wrong?
27. How do I specify arguments for application program execution from the IDE?

ANSWERS

1. Why do I have to create a project?
   A project contains the information about the programs and their dependent files and it also stores and maintains the properties of the IDE. Therefore, to create and run a program, you have to put it in a project.

2. How do I create a Java program?
   There are a number of ways to create a Java program. A simple way is to use the Class wizard. To display a Class wizard, choose *File, New Class*.

3. How do I compile a Java program?
   There are a number of ways to compile a Java program. A simple way is to choose *Make* from the context menu of the program in the project pane.

4. How do I run a Java program?
   There are a number of ways to run a Java program. A simple way is to choose *Run Using Defaults* from the context menu of the program in the project pane.

5. How do I test a Java applet from JBuilder?
   There are a number of ways to test a Java applet. A simple way is to choose *Run* from the context menu of the applet's .html file in the project pane. The applet will be displayed in the applet viewer.

6. How do I delete a file from the IDE?
   Choose *Delete* from the context menu of the file in the project pane.

7. How do I delete a .class file from the IDE?
   Choose *Clean* from the context menu of the .java in the project pane to delete the class for the Java source code. Choose *Clean* from the context menu of the project or package in the project pane to delete the class for the entire project or package.

8. How do I add a file or a package to a project?
   Click the *Add* button in the project pane to display the Add Files or Packages to Project dialog box. You can then select the files or packages to add to the project.

9. How do I remove a file or a package from a project?
   Select the file or package in the project pane and click the *Remove* button in the project pane to remove the selected file or packages.

10. How do I rename a file?
    In the context menu of the file in the project pane, choose *Rename* to display the File dialog box. Rename the file in the File Name field.

11. How do I set the code style to generate the template with the next-line style?
    Choose the Next line option in the Code Style tab of the project Properties dialog box.

12. How do I set the block indent for the Java source code editor?
    The block indent can be specified in the Editor tab of the Editor Options dialog box. By default, it is 2.

13. How do I format the code in JBuilder 7 or higher?
    Highlight the code in the editor and choose the *Format* command from the Edit menu or from the context menu in the content pane.

14. How do I change the color and font in the Java source editor?
Choose *Tools, Editor Option* to display the Editor Options window. You can change the font in the Display tab and change the color in the Color tab.

15. How do I disable code insight?
Choose *Tools, Editor Option* to display the Editor Options window. In the CodeInsight tab, uncheck Auto popup MemberInsight.

16. How do I change the look-and-feel to Motif?
Choose *Tools, IDE Option* to display the IDE Options window. You can change the look-and-feel in the Browser tab.

17. How do I disable audio sound in the IDE?
Choose *Tools, IDE Option* to display the IDE Options window. In the Audio tab, uncheck Audio feedback enabled to disable the audio.

18. How do I get help on Java classes, methods, and keywords?
You can get help from the Help window. But the quick way to get help is to highlight the class, method, or keyword and press F1.

19. How do I view the source code for Java classes in the Java API?
Choose *Search, Find Classes* to display the Find Classes window and type the full class name in the Class name field.

20. How do I search a text in all the source files in the source path?
Choose *Search, Find in Path* to display the Find Path window. Type the text to be searched in the Text to find field, and select Full source path to search the text in all the source files in the source path.

21. How do I generate Javadoc documents?
Choose *Wizards, Javadoc* to display the Javadoc wizard to create Javadoc in JBuilder.

22. How do I create an archive file in JBuilder?
Choose *Wizards, Archive Builder* to display the Archive Builder to create archive in JBuilder.

23. How do I add a database driver in JBuilder?
In the Required Libraries tab of the project properties, display the Select One or More Libraries dialog box. Select the library for the driver. If the driver is not in the library, click the New button to display the New Library wizard. You can create a new library for the driver.

24. How do I enable or disable source package discovery and compilation?
You can enable or disable source package discovery and compilation in the General tab of the project properties dialog box.

25. I tried to run the program from the DOS prompt but got `java.lang.NoClassDef FoundError` exception. What is wrong?
The class file is not found. There are several reasons: (1) the class has not been compiled; (2) the classpath was not set properly—you need to set it to **.;%classpath**%. (3) If the class has a package statement, you didn't invoke it with the full class name, including the complete, package name. For example, if the class path is c:\liang and the package for the class is chapter1, you have to type **java chapter1. ClassName** from the **c:\liang** directory.

26. I tried to run the program from the DOS prompt but got `java.lang.NoSuch`
`MethodFoundError` exception. What is wrong?

The class does not have a *main* method or the *main* method signature is incorrect.

27. How do I specify arguments for application program execution from the IDE?
In the Run tab of the Project property window, click New to display the Runtime
Properties window. Type a new configuration name (e.g., MyConfig1) in the Configuration name field and enter the arguments in the Application parameters
field. Click *OK* to close the Runtime Properties window, and click *OK* to close
the properties dialog box. Run the program by clicking *Run using "MyConfig 1"*
in the context menu of the application program.

Index